Getting
Physical

Getting Physical

An autobiography

Scott Gibbs

EBURY PRESS
LONDON

First published in Great Britain in 2000

1 3 5 7 9 10 8 6 4 2

Copyright © Scott Gibbs 2000

Ebury Press
Random House · 20 Vauxhall Bridge Road · London SW1V 2SA

Random House Australia Pty Limited
20 Alfred Street · Milsons Point · Sydney · New South Wales 2061 · Australia

Random House New Zealand Limited
18 Poland Road · Glenfield · Auckland 10 · New Zealand

Random House South Africa (Pty) Limited
Endulini · 5A Jubilee Road · Parktown 2193 · South Africa

The Random House Group Limited Reg. No. 954009

www.randomhouse.co.uk

Papers used by Ebury Press are natural, recyclable products made
from wood grown in sustainable forests.

A CIP catalogue record for this book is available from the British Library.

ISBN 0 09 187130 1

Designed by Lovelock & Co.

Printed and bound in Great Britain by Mackays of Chatham plc, Chatham, Kent

Contents

Foreword

Ever since I first met Scott on the Lions tour of New Zealand in 1993, we've got on. Maybe it's because I had – and still have – a high regard for him as a player, and that continued easily off the field. He's a good guy to go out and have a few beers with, because not only do you feel protected on the field, you feel very protected off it.

My early memories of Scott are obviously from that Lions tour. He was fairly quiet – until he'd had a few drinks. Then, this quiet, unassuming individual, who sometimes wore glasses, read books and listened to jazz, all of a sudden turned into a totally different person, and the fun side came out. But he is a single-minded guy who knows what he wants to do and what he wants to achieve. After that tour he went back to Wales with a good reputation as a player, but he was so demoralised with what people were saying about the Welsh national team that soon after he left for rugby league. On the outside he seemed like a very confused individual, but once he'd made up his mind, that was it.

I was sure the rugby league guys would have a great deal of respect for him because of the way he ran and hit people. Scott went up there and said, 'Right, I'm going to crack it' – and he did, despite all the criticism from back home. It's brilliant that he was able to go from a career in international rugby union and do so well in rugby league.

Having said that, it's always great to see a good player come back to union, although on a personal note you can't help thinking, Oh my God, if things work out I'm going to be playing against this guy again. There was always the chance that we'd be going one-on-one against each other, although I would certainly never run straight at him. He once told me, 'Don't worry, Jerry, I would never intentionally hurt you. There's no way I would take your head off or anything like that.' Which was reassuring. However, if he was given the opportunity to give me a clean, legal shot I was sure he'd take it, and of course I'd do the same. The difference is, my hit wouldn't have any impact on him.

Playing for England against Wales at Twickenham in 1998, when we beat them 60–26, I remember making a bit of a break and coming into his territory. I felt his presence immediately, and a rush of air went past me – maybe it was a swinging arm. I made sure I ran on a few yards before looking round for support, because if I'd been anywhere in his vicinity I knew I'd get it.

His reputation for being a hard player was enhanced on the 1997 Lions tour to South Africa, and for him to be named Player of the Tour was just an awesome achievement. I don't think anyone on that trip would have disagreed with the choice. During the Test series there was talk of how big and strong the Springbok forwards were, but I remember Scott actually shouting to their forwards, 'Come on! Run at me!' They were so easily provoked that they just kept running at him, and Gibbsy, true to form, kept knocking them down.

I once called Scott 'the fastest prop in the world', and when he hit the twenty-stone bulk of South African prop Os du Randt, he proved himself to be the strongest as well. Du Randt is a pretty brutal individual, but on that occasion Scott just blew him away. When you see something like that with your own eyes, you just shake your head because you're not quite sure whether it's happened or not. Fran Cotton, our tour manager, said it was one of the defining moments of the tour. Even the South Africans gasped as du Randt was bundled over. Scott certainly likes the physical side of things (he's also pretty nimble on his feet, as he showed at Wembley in 1999).

His experiences in rugby league taught him well how to live life as a professional. A lot of his Welsh colleagues and team-mates at Swansea might say, 'I don't quite understand Scott,' but that's because he tends to keep his personal, private life separate from his rugby, which is what being professional is all about. He's very passionate about Swansea and Wales. He might sometimes come across as matter-of-fact, but as long as the guy's giving 100 per cent on the field I don't think you can have a problem with that. Some people say that when Scott pulls up at Swansea or wherever, he gets out of the car and leaves the engine running so he can make a quick getaway. Rugby is thought of as a very sociable game, and there's pressure to conform, but if a player wants to leave and go home to a more comfortable environment, then why not?

Scott, like me, has a passion for his sport which no one will ever understand. I think it's even more difficult for him as a Welshman, because everyone there is expected to be so obviously passionate about the game. I know that Scott's a good guy who on the rugby field will do anything and everything to win. I can't think of anyone I'd rather have alongside me.

He really has established himself over the years as a world-class player, and I think he's one of the few who could walk into any national side. On his day, Scott would be in a World XV, no question. People in rugby all over the world have a very high regard for him, and you can't get a bigger accolade than that.

He's a good player, and I like to think of him as a good friend. They say that when you play rugby you make friends for life. Scott will always be a friend of mine as far as I'm concerned.

Jeremy Guscott
November 1999

CHAPTER ONE

Neath to Wales in Ten Games

My first recollection of rugby is watching it on television at my nan's house. I can't remember how old I was, or who was playing, but I think it was an international. The first game I can recall properly was Wales v. England at the Arms Park in March 1977, and I can still see J.P.R. Williams running down the touchline and handing off Mike Slemen.

I always used to enjoy going to my nan's. I was usually taken there because my dad was going to the game and my mum was going shopping – she never enjoyed rugby much. It was great because my nan always used to slice up oranges for me and put sugar on them. She'd give me lots of little treats like that.

My nan was a massive rugby fan and a season ticket holder at Bridgend, so she would go and watch them every Wednesday night and Saturday. She would also go to Scotland with the nurses from work to watch Wales play, so she was probably more responsible for me getting into rugby than anyone else.

My dad is from Bridgend and my mother from Pencoed, a small village about five miles from Bridgend, which is where we lived. I was born in Pencoed on 23 January 1971. My brother, Simon, was born in 1973 and my sister, Claire, two years later. I was christened Ian Scott Gibbs, and during my childhood my mum and dad always called me Ian. It was my nan who used to call me Scott, and eventually everyone else did too. She had a lot of influence in those early days, even to the point of deciding what kind of schooling we had. My parents didn't speak Welsh, and neither did my grandfather, but my nan was from west Wales and was Welsh-speaking, so she made sure I went to a Welsh school, Dolau primary school, then on to Scholl Llanharry comprehensive. I don't remember much about junior school except that we played rugby in the winter and did athletics in the summer. The kids were fortunate in that the school had acres and acres of fields, and generally I enjoyed my time there.

I was probably about ten when I first showed an interest in rugby. My dad took me along to see a match, but it wasn't until I started playing youth rugby that I really got into the sport. I think Pencoed rugby club was among the first to have a junior section, so I started playing mini rugby there. I enjoyed playing and training, and it was probably also a good excuse for my dad to get out of the house on a Sunday. He was an active man himself, a pole vaulter who had represented Wales. I used to wear his international vest when I did athletics at school. In his scrapbooks there's pictures of him with the likes of Lyn Davies and Ron Pickering, so he must have been pretty good. He played a bit of rugby too, on the wing for Bridgend Sports, but like most people, rugby for him was just a bit of fun followed by a couple of beers afterwards.

Up to the age of sixteen I'd go with him and watch Bridgend at the Brewery Field twice a week. As soon as Wednesday night came round, if Bridgend were at home I knew we'd be off to the rugby. If they were away, we would probably go to the swimming baths. On Saturday it was down to the Brewery Field again, and on Sunday I'd be taken down to Pencoed to play mini rugby. So even at a young age rugby played a big part in my life.

Everyone assumes that because I grew up in the seventies and eighties I must have admired the greats of Welsh rugby, but I got quite disillusioned early on. I would go to Bridgend and ask for autographs, but I got shunned by so many guys it was unbelievable. I can laugh at it now as a child's way of looking at things, but for me, at that time, the true stars were Bridgend players like Mark Titley and Howell Davies because the others didn't seem to have much time for the likes of me. I never saw Gareth Edwards at Bridgend, but I can clearly remember Phil Bennett telling me to get lost. I've met Phil many times since then, and he's a lovely guy, but I don't think I've ever reminded him of that incident. Bridgend had a lot of support in those days so I can imagine it being a very busy place on match day, and I suppose the players didn't want to be pestered by kids. Despite this I have fond memories of those days at Bridgend.

I didn't really enjoy secondary school. I had no idea what I was going to do with my life. I wasn't worried about it, but in lessons I probably didn't try as hard as I should have. I enjoyed games and playing for the school on Saturday mornings, and I quite enjoyed history too. The class was studying the assassination of JFK at one point, and I got quite engrossed in that. I seem to remember I got a B for that paper, but that was about as far as the academic side of things went. Like most people who didn't enjoy school, with hindsight I wish I'd tried harder and gone on to university to do a degree. But then again, when I look around, so many of my friends who went to university have ended up in the police force or the fire brigade, jobs for which you don't really need a degree.

When work really started to matter in school, rugby took over. I had started off playing on the wing, then gradually moved in to stand-off. When I got to secondary school, the coach wanted someone else to play stand-off so I moved into the centre, which didn't bother me at all; I played centre for Pencoed Youth anyway. There wasn't much coaching at that time – we'd have maybe one games lesson a week – and at Pencoed we didn't have any floodlights so we got used to playing touch football in the dark! I played for the school senior team on Saturday mornings and the youth side at Pencoed on Saturday afternoons. I enjoyed playing for the youth team more than the school because it was tougher rugby and you were often up against guys that were eighteen and nineteen rather than fifteen and sixteen. In my time with the youth team I remember being up against the likes of Adrian Davies, who also went on to play for Wales. We had a good side, were well respected in south Wales at that time and won a few cups.

My work at school also suffered because my mother died of cancer when I was fifteen. It was a huge blow for everyone in the family and a terrible shock for me. It came at a time when I was gradually trying to get into rugby and during an important time at school, so I suppose indirectly it had an effect on my attitude. I was bitterly disappointed and distraught for a while, but I slowly got over that. My dad played a big part in my upbringing after that. Earlier on in my life I had spent so much time with my mother and grandmother; I didn't really do anything with my dad except for going to rugby and the swimming baths. When my mum died, my dad was there and he gave up a lot to bring us up, which must have been tough – looking after three kids either coming into or in their teens. We had a full house, and being the eldest I felt a sense of responsibility towards my sister and brother.

We'd all known that mum was ill, but we didn't know it was terminal until the end. I remember my dad taking me to one side one day and telling me. I was probably the closest one to him. I can remember being at my nan's for tea when the phone rang. I knew exactly why it was ringing. I didn't wait to pick up the phone, I just ran straight down the road. It was a traumatic time. I've never seen my dad cry so much.

I played rugby at youth level for two years and was eventually selected for Wales Youth, making my debut against Canada Juniors in October 1988. I also played matches in France and Italy, but I can't remember a great deal about those youth internationals except that we lost in France and we lost to England in Torquay, but then we beat them up in Wrexham when I was captain, which meant a lot to me. At the time the whole experience was a big thing for me. I played with a lot of very talented players in the Welsh youth set-up over that period, but because they didn't apply themselves many just disappeared into club football. I remember Neil Jenkins was in the team, but I can't think of anyone else who made it all the way to full international honours. When you're playing for Wales you think it's the ultimate, but so many players think that when they've reached that level success will be handed to them on a plate later on, and that's just not the case.

I didn't really have any other outside interests during my school days – rugby played such a big part in my life. When you're young and single the next thing you do after playing rugby is go out chasing girls and drinking beer, and that was what the guys liked most about playing youth rugby. You also got to travel, and you were in a safe environment when you were with a club because you had your elders around you. I grew up with guys who were older than me and I got dragged along with them while I was still in school. They all had jobs and a few bob in their pockets, and I wanted to do the same because I was playing with them at weekends. But it wasn't until I was playing first-team football that I realised I was going to need a job because rugby wasn't going to pay for everything.

I left school with just Maths and English and got a job with a double-glazing firm through a friend of my dad's, Garth Alexander. I worked in the glazing department with Garth and a young guy from the valleys, and we made the glass and leaded lights etc. We shared the duties, but I didn't get to cut the glass unless Garth wasn't about. I was now earning enough to give my dad some money and leave a little bit in my pocket for the weekend. I played a couple of games for Pencoed in that year and a couple for Bridgend. In the summer of 1990 I actually went on tour with Bridgend to the USA and played in all their games over there. They were good times, and I played alongside Kevin Ellis just before he went to Warrington.

When I got back to Wales I joined Neath. I really wanted to play for Bridgend, but at that time they couldn't offer me a first-team place and, like many ambitious kids, I probably thought I was better than I really was, although I genuinely believed I could play first-team football. Cardiff had told me that they'd be the judge of when I was good enough to play in the first team, but I wasn't particularly bothered about playing for Cardiff at that time. Neath were a different proposition. They were playing exciting rugby and said they would give me a fair crack of the whip.

It was all very much open, running rugby when I was growing up, whether I was playing mini rugby for the school or at youth level, but when I got to Neath I had a specific remit. They were very forward-oriented and had a very physical style, but that suited me. I've always been a good tackler. From the ages of eight to sixteen I was always the side-stepping guy, tending to avoid contact because I wasn't big enough, strong enough or powerful enough. I never contemplated running into people; I would always look to beat them on the outside for pace. So I had to do other things well to keep my place, and I always made my tackles, put people down and enjoyed it. The opposition perhaps targeted me in those early days because I was the smallest in the backs, but making those tackles kept me on the team sheet.

Gradually my body changed and my responsibility as a player changed and developed accordingly. I got into good habits early on in my career; I saw the need for weight training and weightlifting at an early age. There was a gym in Bridgend run by an ex-powerlifting champion so I was already doing proper exercises and picking up other things along the way. You've got to have the mental attitude to play a physical game. As I said, I have always enjoyed tackling and never felt pain. Neither have I ever felt inferior going into a tackle; I've always felt confident, that everything was going to be on my terms, so Neath's game was not a shock for me.

But being at Neath was a real eye-opener in another sense, because they were really into fitness at that time and were gradually building themselves up into a great club. They were a very fit bunch of lads – in fact, I remember my dad threatening to take me to hospital because he felt I was wasting away with all the work. Glen Ball was coaching Neath when I joined, and training was tough. We only had a couple of sessions in the week and one on a Saturday, but we would constantly be running up and down mountains, then thirty minutes or so playing with a rugby ball and honing our ball skills. In my short career to this point I'd had a rugby ball in my hands all the time, and I remember thinking, When are we going to see the ball? Throughout the summer we'd do miles and miles of running up and around the mountain reservoir, then we'd do hill runs and get back to the pitch and do even more running. But it was a much more professional atmosphere than I'd been used to and I soon got into it and enjoyed it.

Neath won the inaugural Heineken League that year, blowing everyone out of the water, and I got the chance to play in the first team in the first month. I hadn't anticipated that; I thought I'd get a game only every now and then. I'd looked at the fixture list and thought they'd probably pick me against the weaker teams, but on 22 September 1990 I played my first League match, against Abertillery, alongside Allan Bateman because the other centre, Colin Laity, was injured. We won that game, and I thought it was great. Then I read in the paper that Allan had joined Warrington. There had been a certain amount of press speculation, but I didn't have any inkling that he was going. But with Allan gone and Colin still injured, I got to play the next game and the next, and so it went on.

After a few games for Neath I was selected to play for Wales B in Holland, around November time. We had a good trip, won the match and then had an enjoyable time in Amsterdam. After the Wales B game, I can remember my dad ringing me at my friend's house where I'd stayed over. I thought, Christ, what's my dad ringing me for? Is there something wrong? But he just said, 'You're picked for Wales!' I was quite excited and a bit shocked.

Just after Christmas, there was a Five Nations training camp for the full Welsh squad. Four centres had been picked – me, Colin Laity, Mark Ring and Mike Hall – so I thought I might be in with a good shout of making the full international team. During the sessions and the trial game I remember trying to make as few errors as possible and trying to do the best I could. When it came to announcing the team I just sat there with my head down. I knew I wouldn't be upset if I wasn't picked because I wasn't really expecting it, but when they read out my name I just had a tingling all through my body. The first time is always the best time.

So there I was, on 19 January 1991 at the age of nineteen, head to head with Will Carling and Jeremy Guscott at the Arms Park. The signs were a touch ominous for Wales: England hadn't won in Cardiff since 1963 and there was a new regime in the Welsh camp with Ron Waldron as coach. There were also a lot of new faces in the side, the newest of them all being me, Pontypridd's Neil Jenkins, and Newport back-row pair Glen George and Alan Carter. I was playing alongside Mark Ring in the centre, so that was a nice personal milestone, to play with someone I'd enjoyed watching when I was younger. There were six Neath players in the team, including the captain Paul Thorburn, so you had a lot of people saying it was because Ron Waldron was ex-Neath, but I wasn't going to let that hinder me. I was picked and I was ready to give my all.

I quite clearly remember walking down Westgate Street from the Angel Hotel that day. I didn't really know what to expect as it was a massive step up for me, but I knew I was pretty fit and keen to do well. Of course, putting on the Welsh jersey and running out to that incredible noise was an amazing experience. I'd had advice from a lot of people in the team, and it must have been about twenty minutes into the game before I took my eyes off the crowd, because I was just looking around in amazement thinking, This is just like everyone says it is. The sound of the singing was incredible, and I didn't have to wait long for my first touch of the ball, because England kicked off to me. The next thing I knew Dean Richards and all these monsters in white were charging down on me. That was the first and only time someone's kicked off to me at the start of a game, so I was involved from the off. We ended up losing that match 25–6, mainly through indiscipline and the boot of Simon Hodgkinson, the England full-back, who just slotted over the goals. But any time anyone ran at me I put them down, and I was in Carling's face all the time.

That year we managed to draw with Ireland but lost all our other games and ended up with the wooden spoon, but I wasn't disappointed. I was just pleased to be in the team and I was satisfied I had done my best. I must have made an impression because I was voted Welsh Player of the Year for 1990/91, the youngest ever winner apparently. I was elated at the end of the season and had to do a lot of press as well, which was new to me. I didn't have a lot of guidance at the time, and in the following seasons it got a bit much for me. I had also had Wigan on the phone after that first season – the first time any rugby league club had registered an interest in me. Kevin Ellis, Allan Bateman, Rowland Phillips and Mark Jones had all gone north, so there was naturally speculation about me. It was easy news for the papers, I suppose.

I was still working for the glazing firm, so after the euphoria of playing at Cardiff Arms Park against some of the biggest names in the game and then putting on a dinner jacket and mixing with them, I drove back to work on the Monday. Everyone there was fantastic; they were right behind me. Even though Wales didn't win a game that season there were plenty of pats on the back as well as pieces of advice. But I never let it all go to my head. I've always seen rugby as a fun job and I'm always glad when the match is over. I learned at a very young age not to dwell on a game. I saw so many people ruin themselves through wondering about what might have been, but once it's over that's it, there's nothing you can do about it.

I never thought about rugby as a potential career. We got expenses at Neath – I think we had a couple of quid to wash our kit, for example – and would get £10 or £15 if we won at the weekend, so there would be a small cheque every month, but everything was documented and all our tax was paid. I really enjoyed working at the double-glazing firm with Garth and the others, but it was always going to conflict with my rugby commitments. Towards the end of my time with the firm, when I was getting a bit more publicity, they wanted me to go out on the road selling the product, but that didn't last long. I did one job as a double-glazing salesman and found out it wasn't really me. I enjoyed the solitude of the factory more. As soon as I started playing first-team football I would maybe have a day off in the week because of the travelling – but, of course, I needed more extended breaks for trips and tours. Most of the guys at Neath were farmers or had direct career prospects in finance or whatever and it was easier for them to manage their time.

I didn't have any clear career ambitions, so in some respects I was lucky that after about ten games for Neath I was selected to play for Wales B in Holland, and within a few months of that I was winning my first cap against England. Things changed drastically for me that season. I was going places with rugby, and although I enjoyed working there and have many fond memories of the place, by the end of the year I had left the double-glazing firm and gone to work for a television production company in Cardiff, which was a definite career path and enabled me more easily to work alongside my rugby.

I'd already achieved a lot in my short time in top-flight rugby, and I was now poised to move onwards and upwards.

CHAPTER TWO

To Hull
and Back

Apparently, after my first international I said I'd like to retire at twenty-five, which was a bit of a bold statement. I had crammed a lot into that first year and I suppose I'd thought, If it carries on like this I'm probably not going to last much beyond that age. It was a bit of a tongue-in-cheek comment, but still in those early days of my international career, rugby was just a game to me.

At the end of my first season in international rugby, Wales toured Australia, and it turned out to be a real nightmare. The best part of the whole trip was the two flights there and back first class on Qantas. It was my first long-haul trip and it took us twenty-four hours to get there. We played against Perth first and beat them 22–6, but as they were one of the weakest sides we would come up against it didn't really prepare us for what was ahead. The next match was a much tougher proposition, Queensland in Brisbane, and we got beaten 35–24.

I suppose an international tour should be a good experience for a player, but almost from the outset I didn't enjoy it. It was just rugby, rugby, rugby. We'd train every day; even the day before the game we'd be going flat out, then the morning after the game we'd be training again. We never saw anything of the country; all we saw was hotels and rugby pitches. At one point we were just thirty minutes from the Great Barrier Reef, and I thought we'd at least get to spend an afternoon there. But no, we didn't even see a crocodile or any wildlife at all while we were there, we just trained and trained.

It would have been more bearable had we been getting the right results. After Queensland we just managed to beat ACT 7–3 in Canberra in freezing cold weather, but then New South Wales hammered us 71–8 in Sydney, and the only game I didn't play in was the match against Queensland Country, which we won 35–7. The final match on tour, the Test against Australia at the Ballymore Oval in Brisbane, proved the worst disaster. The Aussies, who were to win the World Cup a few months later, were red hot and completely destroyed us. The 63–6 loss was the biggest defeat suffered by a Welsh representative side at that time.

As I said, I didn't enjoy the trip at all, and to cap it all there was great unhappiness within the squad off the field. At that time I was still with Neath, but I had built up a great rapport with the Swansea boys, people like Richard Webster, Robert Jones and Anthony Clement. There was a heavy Neath contingent on the trip and people were again saying that the coach, Ron Waldron, was showing favouritism towards them. This led to animosity among the players, which at one time nearly ended in a scrap in the Brisbane City Travelodge car park. Everyone was picking sides; it was a case of 'Are you with us or with them?' and it got a bit silly. I didn't choose sides, I just stood back and wondered what the hell was going on. Gareth Llewellyn cut his hand – I don't know what happened and I don't want to know really. I just remember standing back and saying, 'Hell boys, what's going on?' Obviously there were a lot of people who had a chip on their shoulder and too much drink in their bellies. Another symptom of the unease within the squad was the infamous bread-roll-throwing dinner scene. It was all ugly and didn't do anything for morale.

That was when Ron started thinking about retiring because he'd had a gutful. He was having health problems through the stress and it was a pretty traumatic time for everyone really. There wasn't enough resolve in the squad to bring us all together because we were getting hammered on the pitch and everyone was pointing the finger at everyone else, from their team-mates to Ron and all the coaching staff. The players were saying that the whole thing was ridiculous and asking why they couldn't have a day off and enjoy themselves, and then the skipper, Paul Thorburn, was having a go at the boys for going out on the piss and not eating the right foods etc. There were massive personality clashes on that tour; everyone thought they knew the way forward. When you're away in another country for a month, you've got to have a happy camp, and our camp certainly wasn't happy.

I remember on one occasion, when we were staying at the Manly Pacific Hotel, a couple of players came in with lollipops in their mouths. Ron saw them and went bananas. His view was that we were supposed to be a mature international rugby team, yet here were two players eating little lollipops. He embarrassed me, too, one night because he got me up on a table and asked me to strip off in front of everyone, saying to the forwards, 'If this twelve-stone bastard can run all day and tackle, why can't you?' It was flattering in a way, because he referred to me as 'a little battleship', but the episode showed I was definitely trying on that tour and getting stuck in. In his eyes I wasn't giving up, and maybe he thought all the others just didn't give a damn.

Clive Rowlands, who was Robert Jones's father-in-law, was manager on that trip and he tried to steady the camp. Everyone had his own point of view, and I can tell you it wasn't a nice situation to be in at the age of twenty – there were only a few younger guys who I'd played with for the Welsh Youth side, like Luc Evans. The medical staff were also having a go at a lot of the boys about faking injuries just so they could get out of training. It was boiling hot in Brisbane, and because we were training on hard grounds, everyone had shin splints. We also weren't eating correctly because some of the places we stayed in just weren't up to scratch. In the first place we stayed just outside Fremantle, Cottesloe Beach, all the beds were damp. There were cockroaches and lice everywhere, and the food was non-existent. The guys were ordering pizza because we were just not eating enough. We'd run the three miles to training with Ron in the charabanc behind just wagging his finger. We'd get to the training pitch and then run eight laps to warm up. We'd be really knackered and then be expected to play. I don't think we had one rest day during that whole trip. It was unbelievable.

One of the few good things was that I met up with Jonathan Davies, who was out there playing rugby league for Canterbury Bankstown. From a young age Jonathan had been quite an influential figure. He had signed for Widnes in January 1989, and when all the rumours started about me switching to rugby league he gave me some good advice. He came over one night and we had a couple of beers with a friend of mine from Pencoed, so I probably did have one or two good times on that tour, but there weren't very many. It was my first and my last Welsh tour.

When we got back Ron Waldron, unsurprisingly, handed in his

notice, and so did Paul Thorburn, so we were immediately plunged into a new regime: Alan Davies and Bob Norster. At the start of the new season, 1991/92, we had a warm-up game against France, the first floodlit game to be held at Cardiff Arms Park. The French won 22–9. Then we were into the World Cup, in a group that included Western Samoa, Australia and Argentina. We were now a happier bunch, there were new squad members and things were a little bit better, and we were based up at the St Pierre golf club in Chepstow, which was a good training camp. We thought we'd definitely qualify as runners-up.

Looking back, you wouldn't have thought there was a World Cup on in Wales, or even Britain, because I can't remember any hype or buzz about the competition. Our first game was against Western Samoa, and we were in for a shock. They were big South Sea islanders, very physical, and they really laid into us. Phil May dislocated his shoulder, Anthony Clement broke his ribs and I got a short arm in my face, so the three of us ended up in Cardiff Royal Infirmary. We ended up losing 16–13, and after the game we just sat there, very disappointed.

I remember having a scuffle with Frank Bunce, the Samoan centre who later went on to play for the All Blacks. Personally, I didn't find it too physical, but there were some massive hits in that game. I don't think we expected them to be that up front because we thought, Western Samoa, who are they? They were still something of an unknown quantity, but when you think that Frank Bunce, Junior Paramore, Pat Lam and Apollo Perelini were playing in that game, all of whom have gone on to make a name for themselves in top-flight rugby, I suppose it wasn't that surprising.

In the Welsh camp everyone was just making excuses again – each new regime seemed to bring its ups and downs. We managed to beat Argentina 16–7, which improved the atmosphere a bit, but then we played Australia and lost 38–3, and I seemed to spend the whole game tackling the Australian full-back Marty Roebuck. I took a bang on my knee late in the game and went off, and I remember wondering if it was all worth it. I'd won just once at Test level out of the nine games I'd played for Wales that calendar year. The press were getting on our backs, so the enjoyment of playing for Wales at that time was pretty limited. We were all getting just as much stick as each other in the end. They were being quite easy on the younger boys, but I was finding that the Welsh press was very scathing and I genuinely thought to myself, If this carries on much longer I may as well take the money and switch to rugby league. I'd be better off playing for a living rather than giving my all and getting sod all. Everywhere we went people just didn't want to know us, and there weren't many people putting up their hands and saying, 'I want to play for Wales.' The only solace was back at club level, where you could really enjoy your rugby.

I also changed jobs around this time. Just before the World Cup I met Martyn Williams, an ex-television producer who had set up an independent production company called Rugby Vision, dealing mainly in Welsh-language television, which he ran with his partner, Lesley. They were also producing a magazine for the Welsh Rugby Union called *Dragon News*. I got to know Martyn when I and a few other players were doing some commercial work on behalf of the WRU. He offered me a job as a researcher because he was doing some work for ITV during the World Cup. Martin was very good to me, giving me an opportunity to get a different outlook on rugby and develop a career. I was working on the teams in the World Cup, which involved things like getting pen portraits together and information on all the players. I was working opposite the Welsh Rugby Union offices on Westgate Street in Cardiff, so just about every press opportunity that came along, they used me. It made perfect sense as I was the most accessible, so I was in the news all the time, either marketing the World Cup or featuring in *Dragon News*, and at the time I thought it was great.

I was with Martyn for a couple of years, and during that time he was more like a father figure to me than a boss because he used to give me good advice. When the rugby league offers came in we sat down and talked things through, and he'd give me his impartial view. He knew exactly the right thing to do. I look back on my time with Rugby Vision with fond memories. If you talk to anyone in television, they'll tell you the hardest part is just getting in, but thanks to Martyn I was already there. There was a career path from researcher to production assistant, manager, producer etc., and at that time Rugby Vision had a Welsh production called *Wales's Strongest Man*, so I worked a little bit on that while contributing to the *Dragon News* editorial. It obviously helped that I was Welsh-speaking myself, although my Welsh has never been great. Obviously you get better the more you speak it, and there were a lot of players in the Welsh squad at that time who were Welsh-speaking, so I improved.

However, I slowly grew to resent being in the public eye all the time, probably because I'd had so much of it from a young age. I was doing so much I could have filled twenty scrapbooks with pictures and articles, and I was getting fed up with seeing my own face in the press. At the beginning of 1992, I wanted to escape from it all.

The Five Nations championship was on us again, and Wales were due to play Ireland first. I was getting some stick and becoming depressed and wasn't even enjoying my club rugby. We were in the training camp a week and a half before the Irish international, and during that time I took a call late one night from

Dave McKnight, who is a rugby agent. He said he'd got a deal with Hull rugby league club which was really good and I really should go for it. It came right out of the blue, and I was on my own. I didn't even have my dad with me. Dave showed me the figures. I was feeling down and a bit impulsive. At that time I didn't know whether I was going to get picked for Wales again as I didn't think I was playing that well, so I said, 'Yes.' Dave asked me to meet him the following day at Knutsford services on the M6, where we'd meet the Hull chairman, Steve Watson.

When my dad came back and I told him I was going to sign for Hull, he said he thought I was doing the wrong thing, but the next day I got out of training with the Welsh squad by telling them I had flu and then I shot up the motorway. The M6 seemed to go on for ever, and when I eventually got to the Knutsford services I looked for Dave but couldn't find him. I remember looking at a map and seeing where Hull was. I couldn't believe how much further it was, so I thought, Sod this, and got back in my car and headed home. I drove back really fast in a bit of a panic, thinking, What am I going to do now? Dave was going to be pissed off with me, as was Steve Watson, and my old man wasn't going to be too chuffed either.

When I got back to south Wales I went to the training camp at Cowbridge. I had my long Drizabone stockman's coat on and sniffled a bit to make it seem like I did have the flu. After the session I went back to the team hotel and up to my room. Suddenly, the phone went. It was Steve Watson. He said, 'Where are you, Scott?' When I told him I was in Cardiff he told me to stay there and said they were on their way down to sign me. I said, 'Steve, I'm not signing for Hull today or tomorrow, I'm stopping here.' He said he had Dave McKnight with him and that he wasn't too pleased with me as I hadn't done his reputation much good with my coming and going.

A lot has been said in the rugby league press about this incident. I knew Mark Jones was at Hull and I thought it would be all right, but when I joined St Helens later they said it wouldn't have been a good move for me because Hull at that time were a struggling team. Also, I didn't have any lawyers with me that day so I could have been signing away the next ten years of my career. I'd been doing a lot of soul-searching, but I finally saw sense and thought that things could only get better. I reckoned that if I was still playing well in Wales, rugby league would still want me – if I wanted to go.

I did get into the Welsh team, and we started off the Five Nations in a more positive way, managing to beat Ireland 16–15 at Lansdowne Road. But after that we were beaten by France in Cardiff 12–9 and lost 24–0 to England at Twickenham. We were under pressure in that game, and I remember I was just tackling for the whole match. We ended on a high with a 15–12 victory over Scotland at home, so even though we didn't have a great Five Nations, we at least played a bit more football and didn't get too much stick from the press.

I had switched clubs in January 1992, moving from Neath to Swansea. After my first season at Neath, some of the Welsh Rugby Union aficionados had said that if I wanted to develop my international career I'd have to make a move because the style at Neath didn't suit me and it was going to hinder my progress. After winning the championship Neath went very forward-oriented and almost always played ten-man rugby. I had a specific remit in that team which was to bottle up the midfield rather than do anything creative. I was still trying my hardest, but it was becoming very frustrating because I was hardly touching the ball. I was running my bollocks off in training, but when the game came around I wasn't seeing the ball. Mike Ruddock, the coach from Swansea, rang me and said, 'You seem to get on well with the boys, and Anthony Clement and Richard Webster speak highly of you, so we'd really like to have you at Swansea.' I told him I had to be fair to Neath and said I'd give it another go. But it still wasn't working out, so I rang Mike back and we met at the services at Bridgend. We chatted for a while, and I agreed to join them.

It wasn't just me who was feeling stifled at Neath. Adrian Davies felt the same, and we believed that the type of football the team was playing was detrimental to our rugby and affecting our wider ambitions. So Adrian and I went to Alan Benjamin, the club secretary, and asked for a transfer. I had a face-to-face meeting with Glen Ball and the club officials, and they couldn't believe I wanted to move, but there was little they could do about it because I wasn't contractually obliged to them. Rugby was still an amateur sport. We did get expenses, of course, and if we won we'd get £60, which the club paid tax on, but it was hardly a fortune. Some of the guys would toss coins or turn cards in the changing room in an effort to increase their share. The £60 would fund your weekend, and it was nice at the end of the game, particularly when it had been lashing down, to know that you had a few quid in your pocket. But money was never my motivation to switch clubs. When I spoke to Mike, and he asked me why I wanted to come to Swansea, all I said was, 'I want to be a better player.'

Adrian ended up joining Cardiff, and I joined Swansea, which turned out to be the best move I ever made because they had a totally different view on things. Whereas Neath spent so much time slogging away in training with not a rugby ball in sight, at Swansea they were really into playing football and the players had a lot more footballing ability. We did a lot of skills and drills in training and a lot less conditioning. I found that almost overnight

I became a better player simply through being around better players and just handling the ball more.

The move came at the right time for me. I wasn't enjoying my rugby at Neath, and playing for my country was frustrating. I seemed to be trying my best and getting nowhere, so the move to Swansea was crucial. Swansea have always played attractive rugby, and in my first game for them – against Cardiff – I scored a hat-trick, so that proved to me I'd done the right thing. I touched the ball so many times and was scoring tries just through supporting players. I was getting the ball more and seemed to be in the right place at the right time, so right from the off I thoroughly enjoyed myself.

But I have to take my hat off to Neath because it was a very friendly club and they made everyone feel welcome. My dad enjoyed his time at Neath, and even now, when you speak to anyone who has played for Neath they all say that's the best club they've played for.

While everything on the field was great at Swansea, off the field they were a bit more stand-offish. My father didn't feel at all comfortable in that environment because they never really welcomed him into the family. Swansea are more of a city club; everyone seems more independent, and they don't have that warmth you get at some of the other clubs. At Swansea there are a lot of committee men – people in blazers – and even though I've been there for six seasons in all now, I still don't know all their names. But it was without a doubt the best move for me rugby-wise.

In February after I made my debut for Swansea, we played against Transvaal, who were over in Britain on tour, and I met up with their president and chief executive. South Africa were slowly getting back into world rugby, and they asked me to go and play for them during our summer. They also asked Robert Jones, so we were both looking forward to it, but I'd picked up an injury during the World Cup. I had a cyst and a ganglion on my knee which required an operation, and I had to have that done during the summer, which meant I missed out on the trip to South Africa. Robert also missed out for some reason, although he went a couple of years later. I was really disappointed because it was an opportunity to learn about different styles, express myself more and improve my game, benefiting Swansea in the process. But we won the championship at Swansea in 1992 anyway, which was great.

There was a club tour to Canada later that summer which I wasn't going to go on because I'd still be recovering from my knee operation. But Mike Ruddock said, 'Come along anyway; you can use it as part of your training regime,' which sounded like a great idea. So I went. And then, of course, I ended up playing. Another rugby season had gone by in a flash.

CHAPTER THREE

Trial by Taxi

The highlight of the first half of the 1992/93 season was Swansea beating Australia 21–6 on 4 November at St Helen's. The Wallabies were touring Ireland and Wales and, certainly on the Welsh leg, the rain seemed to follow them around. Every game seemed to be played in a downpour, and our match against them at St Helen's was no exception. It was a Wednesday, and there was a gale-force wind blowing to boot, but there was still some good football played and we beat them convincingly. It was a tremendous win, and when I look back, I think that was the best Swansea side I'd played in up until then. It was a historic day. Many will say it was the club's best ever, and there's a photograph hanging up in the clubhouse to commemorate the event.

We didn't do so well in the Test, though, the Wallabies winning 23–6, which didn't augur well for the 1993 Five Nations. We kicked off on 6 February by beating England 10–9 at Cardiff Arms Park. It was great; we put in a terrific defensive effort and showed lots of character. Gareth Edwards compared it to Rorke's Drift, and everybody thought that at last we'd turned the corner. But we came down to earth with a bump in our very next match, against Scotland at Murrayfield. We were beaten 20–0 and were never in it. Ireland beat us 19–14 in the next game at Cardiff, and then France blew us away in Paris. The rugby always seemed to be played at a different pace at the Parc des Princes. They beat us 26–10 to take the championship while we ended up with the wooden spoon.

To add to my frustrations, Alan Davies, the coach, started saying that he wasn't sure whether I was an inside centre or an outside centre as it was his view that the inside centre was usually the decision-maker and ball player. It was only when I went on the Lions tour that I played inside centre, and I really enjoyed it. In fact I learned more from Ian McGeechan in those nine weeks than I did from all my coaches up until that time.

At the beginning of the season I hadn't really given the Lions tour to New Zealand much thought. It was only when we played France in our last Five Nations match and the following week they were due to pick the Lions tour party that it crossed my mind. I remember thinking that it must be great going on a Lions tour, because in 1989 when they were in Australia I used to go back to a friend's house and be gripped by the games on TV. I didn't imagine for one minute that I'd be picked for the 1993 tour. I thought Robert Jones would probably go because he was on the last one, and people like Mike Hall, but there had been no indication that I was being considered. I didn't even know exactly when they were announcing the squad until I got a phone call from John Kennedy of the *Western Mail.*

'What do you think of the news?' he said.

'What do you mean, John?' I replied.

'You've been picked for the Lions.'

He said the party had just been announced on Radio Five Live, but I still found it hard to believe. I hadn't been waiting by the phone or listening to the radio or anything. It all came as a total shock.

Then Kennedy repeated his question: 'What do you think?'

I said, 'From now on I'm just going to try to keep fit and free from injury and make sure I'm on that plane. I'll worry about the playing side of things when I get there. I haven't had as much experience as these guys but I'll give it my best shot.'

John said he needed a photograph of me and all the other Welshmen in the squad, and asked if I could make it that afternoon, so I drove over to Sophia Gardens and we all had our photograph taken together.

Of course my old man was ecstatic, and everyone was euphoric. Dai Richards, one of the Lions selectors, rang me about half an hour after John Kennedy and wished me all the best. But my participation in the Lions tour was to hang by a thread due to an incident which threatened to mar my career.

In April, over the Easter weekend, the World Cup Sevens were on in Scotland. I was laid low, full of flu, and wasn't able to go. I had been feeling really bad all weekend but got fed up of being in the house, so on Sunday I went out for lunch to the White Horse in Coychurch with a few mates and had a couple of pints. I never usually drank beer, but on that occasion I had a couple of pints of Brains Bitter and played some cards. Then we went into town, and that's when things just got a bit out of hand.

I hadn't eaten much for about two days and had probably had a bit too much to drink, so I was just a bit the worse for wear. We went to the taxi rank and ordered a taxi, but the woman said, 'You'll have to wait, there aren't any taxis.' She was a bit curt with me, although after the incident she accused me of being abrupt, but I've never been like that. So we walked out and I noticed the keys in the ignition of one of the taxis outside. They must have been glinting at me, and I was joking with my friends when on impulse I just jumped in and drove off. I'd only gone about fifty yards down the road when I realised I'd done something wrong, but by then it was too late. We heard over the radio that a taxi had been stolen, and the location was given. As I pulled out, there was a convoy of taxis behind me, and when I stopped at the traffic lights opposite the police headquarters one of them cut me off. We all got out of the car immediately and I went to the taxi behind me to apologise, but he must have thought I was coming across to have a go because he wound his window up.

We knew we'd done wrong, and were very apologetic. We hadn't done any damage, so I thought nothing of it and we just walked off past the South Wales Police HQ and through the industrial estate. But soon I could hear sirens, and I thought, We're in the shit now. We hid in bushes and behind lorries on the industrial estate, and when we thought they'd gone we slowly started to emerge from our hiding places. I thought, Okay, I've stolen something. I shouldn't have driven away but no harm's been done. I've only driven it down the road and I stopped at the red lights. I wasn't terrorising anyone. Yes, I could have hit someone, but I knew exactly what I was doing even though I knew it was wrong.

Eventually we got to a phonebox on the industrial estate, and ironically enough I was going to ring for a taxi to come and pick us up. But as soon as I reached it a police officer with an Alsatian walked up. The policeman happened to be Steve Sutton, the ex-Wales lock forward, whom we knew. He asked if we were the three boys who had stolen a taxi, and I said, 'Yeah, Steve. Sorry. Can you let us go?' He replied, 'Scott I'd love to, but I can't.' He said he was with his sergeant so he couldn't even if he wanted to. So that was that: the three of us were nabbed.

When the police car pulled up there was another rugby guy driving it, and he said, 'What have you done now?' When we got back to the police station the desk sergeant was a guy from Pencoed who knew my mother. It was all getting a bit embarrassing for me. I was breathalysed and found to be over the limit – not drastically, but I'd broken the law and that was that. Again we admitted what we'd done, even though the woman at the taxi place hadn't recognised me and had only given a description. But there was no point in trying to deny it. After that we spent the night in the cells, which wasn't a pleasant experience. We were all crying; it's not the sort of place you want to be in.

In the morning, Colin Hillman, another rugby player, poked his head in and said, 'What have you been up to?' But the police were very good and didn't rough us up or give us a hard time over the incident. They probably knew it had been a bit of high jinks and we didn't really mean to steal the taxi. When we were charged and they were asking about a date for the court appearance, I had to tell them that I was supposed to go on the Lions tour in May and asked if it could be before then.

When we left the police station the media had gathered outside, so the unpleasantness of the situation continued. I felt awful when I got home, and my dad was the same. We were really stressed out because all these people were camped outside the house. I was convinced I'd really ruined things.

Dai Richards rang and said he'd spoken to the tour manager, Geoff Cooke, and Ian McGeechan, the coach, and he told me not to worry. 'Just do what you need to do,' he said, and I thought, Thank God for that. Swansea supported me as well, but the press were terrible. The *Sun* was the worst: I was on the back page as well as page three. You'd have thought I'd killed someone the way they were going on. They really sensationalised things.

The next few weeks were pretty traumatic because I tried to keep my head down but everyone wanted a piece of me and I had to make an official statement. Richard Webster rang me up and said I could stay round his house for a week or so, and he came round and picked me up. I stayed with him and just tried to keep a low profile until the court appearance. In the meantime I spoke to a lawyer, but there was no getting out of it: I'd broken the law, the case had to proceed. My best chance was to hope that they would be as lenient as possible because at that time I was self-employed and doing some promotional work for Welsh Water, so I really needed my car.

About a month elapsed between the date of the offence and the hearing, so they just managed to get it in before the Lions tour began. What disappointed me about the proceedings was that Steve Sutton didn't tell the truth. He said that on approaching me he had asked whether I had stolen a taxi, and I'd replied, 'No, not me.' I thought that was unfair, and I'm sure it went against me. Sure enough, I was banned from driving for twenty-four months. I thought it was really going to affect me, and I wondered how I was going to survive. I really felt as though everyone was ganging up against me. To cap it all I was also fined nearly £3,000, and when I left the court there were cameras everywhere. On the way out Richard Webster accidentally ran over a cameraman's foot and the BBC used that to get me to do an interview for them. I told them it was Richard, not me, who had been driving, but they said, 'It was your car and we'll have to report it like that,' so they came to the house for the interview and of course they asked me questions about my behaviour etc. I answered them all as honestly as possible and tried to play it all down.

When I got to the Lions camp I thought that what had happened was going to go against me there too, that they'd think I was a right nutcase, but as soon as I walked through the door of the hotel in Weybridge, Dick Best, Geech's assistant coach, told some joke about a taxi, and everyone started ribbing me. I ended up telling the story a thousand times to just about everyone there. But the incident with the taxi had definitely tarnished things for me, and I was determined to keep my head down on tour.

As an exercise in team bonding, we were split up into four teams – A, B, C and D – and I was in the B team along with Will Carling. Dewi Morris had T-shirts printed for each team, and ours was a bit of a piss-take because there was a cartoon on it of a taxi and a policeman waving his truncheon which said THE TAXI DRIVERS DRINKING TEAM. We had to have our photograph taken with our T-shirts on because the guy who had printed them wanted to put them up on his wall. It was a picture that would come back to haunt me.

I was the youngest on the Lions trip, and although it felt very special I was a bit intimidated by everyone. In the first couple of days they issued us with our kit and went through all the other stuff. They said it was going to be a hard job, that New Zealand was the home of the toughest rugby in the world, but I was really looking forward to it. Slowly the memory of the taxi incident was fading, but I still had to be careful. There had been a big debate as to who was going to be captain: Will Carling or Gavin Hastings. I was determined to keep a low profile in this matter because I knew that if someone from the large press contingent saw me playing up on any issue I might get some stick.

It was my first time in New Zealand. We trained hard and I listened to lots of good advice from people like Scott Hastings, Jerry Guscott and Will Carling. Of course Geech (Ian McGeechan) was pointing me in the right direction too, as was Rob Andrew and Stuart Barnes. Every time I played there was experience around me, so it was very good for my rugby. Geech was very personable with his coaching and very attentive as well; pointing me in the right direction position-wise, he would say things like, 'This is what I'd like to do and this is what we're trying to get together to do.' He didn't ignore the fact that I was still young and hadn't had as much experience as the other three centres – who at that time were thirty to forty caps into their international careers – so I enjoyed the experience.

But we didn't get off to a good start. First stop was Paihia in the Bay of Islands on North Island, and I was sharing a room with Dean Richards. There was a thunderstorm and all the electrics went out, so when we woke up in the morning there was no hot water, no heating, no hot coffee. The day was very cold, and I remember Geech sitting us down and saying, 'In 1977 it pissed down for four months, so let's accept it and get on with it.' During that first week we trained in Paihia for our first game, against North Auckland. I wasn't picked for this one, which I was glad about, because I wanted to see for myself how tough it was and how the other guys went. Scott Hastings and Jerry Guscott were the centres in that first match, so that meant that Will Carling and I would probably play in the next one. I assumed he'd want to play inside centre, so I'd have to have a go at outside centre, but I didn't have a problem with that.

After just thirty seconds Ian Hunter broke his collar bone and had to go home. I thought, Bloody hell, what a start! But we won fairly comfortably, 30–17. Anthony Clement had a nightmare of a game, so I had to console him afterwards because his head had gone down. On the other hand Richard Webster had a great game, and both centres had cracking games, so the pressure was on me.

Scott Hastings scored a try, Jerry was brilliant, while Ieuan Evans and the rest of the backs had put on a good show.

So now it was the rest of the squad's turn against North Harbour, who were a different kettle of fish. They had a lot of bigger names in their team, but we had a bigger pack and the game went very well for us, even though there was a bit of a scuffle among all the forwards and the press immediately jumped on the bandwagon saying we were thugs. The final scoreline read 29–13. It was good to get a game under my belt, I was really happy playing alongside Will Carling and Stuart Barnes, and I felt I could relax a little bit because I'd been very nervous.

We maintained our one hundred per cent record by beating the New Zealand Maoris 24–20, but in my next match against Canterbury at Lancaster Park things got a bit sticky. Within five minutes of the kick-off I got smacked in the face, and the next thing I knew it was half-time. I remember literally waking up at half-time as we were all standing in a circle. It was an incredible, surreal experience. I'd never been concussed before, and I just couldn't remember a thing. Jerry Guscott was next to me, Ben Clarke was on my right, and for a few moments I didn't know where I was. I looked up at the scoreboard and it said CANTERBURY V. BRITISH LIONS. I looked around me, looked at the jersey and thought, Jesus, there's Jeremy Guscott and that's Ben Clarke, and I've got a red Lions shirt on. I thought I was in a dream.

The team doctor, James Robson, came over to me and said, 'Are you all right?'

'I don't know where the hell I am,' I replied. 'Am I playing for the Lions?'

'Yes.'

'Are we winning?'

'Yes. You broke through, passed it to Ben Clarke, then to Jerry, and we scored.'

I couldn't remember any of it.

'Scott,' he continued, 'if I take you off now you'll have to get on the next plane home.'

I didn't have a clue what he was on about, but I had the presence of mind to say, 'I'll be all right. Give me time, give me time.'

After that, things slowly started to come back to me. I knew exactly what the scenario would be if I went off with concussion: it's a mandatory three weeks off, so I would have to go home. Towards the latter part of the game I realised where I was. Of course in the changing room afterwards I had a thumping headache. Geech knew the story, but I said, 'I'm fine, I'm all right. Don't put me down as concussed, I've had a bang.' But it was an experience that really frightened me. It was as if I'd just landed in my jersey and my boots from another planet.

The amazing thing was that after getting the knock, as the doc said, I had burst up the middle and passed it to Ben Clarke, who passed it on to Jerry for a score. I didn't have any recollection of that until I watched the video afterwards. I did, however, remember Tony Underwood and Rob Andrew scoring, helping us to win the game 28–10. It was a good victory, but I was feeling so rough afterwards.

We suffered our first defeat of the tour in the next match, going down 37–24 to Otago, so there was a lot of pressure on us in the next game I played in, which was against Southland in Invercargill. It was freezing cold down there and I played in the centre with Tony Clement that day. He needed a big game because his confidence was shot and everyone was ribbing him about his nightmare game against North Auckland. We won 34–16, but I picked up an injury which put my whole tour in jeopardy. Tony

Underwood broke through, passed to me and I caught it in mid-air, but I landed awkwardly on my ankle. The doctor said to me, 'The worst scenario is that it's broken and that will be it,' but we went to the hospital and thankfully it wasn't – just ligament damage and some bruising. That usually means a three-week lay-off, but the medical staff – James Robson and Kevin Murphy – said on this occasion, 'If you do as we tell you and we go at it one hundred miles an hour, you could be back sooner.' I had absolutely no chance of being considered for the First Test, but I had about a week to get fit for the game after that against Taranaki. Geech issued an ultimatum: 'If he doesn't come through the Taranaki game he's got to go home.'

I was very disappointed, because up until the injury everyone was saying, 'Gibbsy, you're in with a shout of being selected for the First Test.' Instead, I watched that First Test up in the gantry with Radio Cymru, and we ended up losing by a narrow margin, 20–18. I felt we had been robbed of a victory, and everyone else felt the same; we'd just about done enough to win. We were all really fed up, but I had other things to concentrate on. I knew that if I didn't come through the midweek game against Taranaki I was on my way home.

I wasn't able to train until the day before the game because my ankle was so heavily strapped, but I was really worked on: I had ice and treatment, more ice and treatment, then some rehab in the pool. Kevin and Dr Robson were very thorough and professional, and a three-week injury was thankfully sorted out in one. It just shows what you can do with proper food and facilities, and tender loving care. Scott Hastings wasn't so lucky: he had had his face smashed in against Otago and was on his way home, and Ireland's Vinnie Cunningham was travelling to New Zealand as a replacement. The only two centres who were fit were Jerry and

Will, and I assumed Geech would stick with them for the Tests.

I was playing alongside Vinnie Cunningham in the centre for the Taranaki game, which was a tough one, but I managed to make a burst which resulted in Damien Cronin scoring. The Lions won the game 49–25. I came through the game unscathed, and my ankle felt fine. I didn't need any injections; just heavy strapping got me through. I was picked for the Auckland game the following Saturday, which we also won 23–18, and that one went well for me too. At least it must have done, because I was voted Man of the Match by the Auckland supporters club, a welcome award I didn't find out about until much later.

I can remember Geech calling me to his room before the side for the Second Test was announced, but I had no idea what he wanted. When I went in I noticed a number twelve jersey on the bed, nicely folded up. Geech sat me down and said, 'You don't know how much pleasure it gives me to hand you this jersey. You've deserved it. You've worked very hard for it.' It was a nice surprise, and a great moment.

The best thing about my selection was that my father was there to see me play. I'd put him through some bad times and a lot of unnecessary stress just before the tour began, so as the date for leaving for New Zealand virtually coincided with my dad's birthday, I decided to pay for him to come out. He came with Richard Webster's dad, Bill, and was there for the last two weeks of the tour.

I don't think even my dad thought I would get into the Test side with the likes of Carling and Guscott there. In fact, when I got to Geech's room I thought he was going to say something like, 'Well done for Saturday, Gibbsy. Is your ankle all right?' A lot of people talk about him being a great coach, which he is, but he's also a lovely person. He didn't have to do what he did; he could have just announced the side and shook my hand. Inviting me to his room to tell me in person was a nice touch; it made me grow inside. Geech always says to new Lions that when you put the shirt on you grow, and it's true. You do feel a kind of metamorphosis – a bit like the Incredible Hulk, really. You feel much stronger, a better player.

Of course the pressure was on the Lions, because we'd lost the First Test and conditions weren't good for the second one. But we really played well that day and beat them 20–7 – one of the great Lions victories. In the last five minutes the All Blacks were really on the rampage, and the clock didn't seem to be ticking down at all, but we kept them out. I can remember afterwards just running across to the boys, and everybody hugging and shouting, 'I love you! I love you!' The only other time I've experienced that level of emotion on a rugby field was after the Challenge Cup final with St Helens in 1996.

That Second Test was a massive game for us; the tactics were sound, and we defended really well. It wasn't a classic game, but if you're down in Wellington and it's lashing down and windy you're not going to see a classic. Discipline played a big part in it, and our kicking went very well. I can't remember many details about the game. I made a little burst, but there was no support and I ended up passing to one of the All Blacks. But all in all I really got stuck in. It was a good day, a good victory. After that game I think the squad was quietly confident that if we played to the best of our abilities we would win the Third Test and take the series. We felt we were in control, and the Third Test was to be played at Eden Park, and you couldn't wish for a bigger, better stadium to play in to cap it all off.

Of course the more experienced players, like the Hastings brothers, Robert Jones and Dean Richards, were advising caution. They had found themselves in the same position on the 1989

Lions tour, needing to win the last to secure a series victory – which they did. We thought we were going to do it as well when we found ourselves 10–0 up in the first ten minutes. I scored a try, and Gavin converted it and then kicked a penalty, but then we gave a couple of tries away and turned round at half-time 14–10 down. If only we could have held on, but a couple of crucial scrums went their way and a couple of plays didn't go our way, and we ended up losing 30–13. It had been a tough run-up to the Third Test, as it always is in New Zealand, particularly so because a fortnight before, the Auckland game at Eden Park had been very physical and fast. The All Blacks didn't seem as intimidating at Lancaster Park and Wellington, but at Eden Park they were something else. Perhaps they thought that if they didn't pull it out now, they would really suffer.

Despite the disappointment, the playing experiences on tour were brilliant. I was offered the opportunity to stay on and play for Waikato, which again was flattering, but having played a whole domestic season and then been on tour for nine weeks – the longest I'd ever been away – I just wanted to get home and forget about rugby for a while. Everywhere we went in New Zealand we were welcomed. It was a great place and the people were lovely, but you just couldn't get away from it.

The only sour note was struck when someone got hold of the photograph of our team wearing those T-shirts, and while we were still on tour it all blew up. The next thing we knew, we had all these drink-drive campaigners on our backs. I was bombarded by journalists and ended up having to answer for the T-shirts' message. My main defence was that we never wore them in public. Yes, ours were offensive, and I'm sure there was material on the other guys' T-shirts that no one wanted to see too, but they were meant to be a private thing for the groups in the squad. But there was a big anti-drink-drive campaign going on at the time, led to a certain extent by Greg Alexander, the Australian rugby league player whose brother had been killed by a drunk driver. The taxi incident was dredged up again and the media began to ask me questions like, 'Whose idea was the T-shirts? Don't you think it's sick? Why are you trying to sensationalise this? Do you know how many hundreds of people are killed or injured because of drunk drivers?' I don't know whether it was used as a ploy to try to unsettle us before the Third Test, but I certainly could have done without it.

But overall, as I said, my trip was pretty good. This was the first tour I'd been on since the 1991 experience in Australia with Wales, and I was just hoping it wasn't going to be like that. It wasn't. We were given opportunities for a bit of rest and relaxation in the first week in Paihia, and I went scuba diving with Peter Winterbottom. I got to know a lot of the other older guys like Mike Teague and Dean Richards by spending a bit of time with them, and I kind of matured as a man and a rugby player. They weren't the three easiest guys to get along with, but I think I earned their respect as the tour went on because I was prepared to put my body on the line. Peter Winterbottom is still one of the best players I've ever played with. He would be so full of cuts his face would look like a map of the M62, yet he'd just keep going. So I got to spend a lot of quality time with quality people, which made me realise that a Lions tour is a lovely environment to play in, a great experience and a great honour.

It's funny. When I came back from the tour, everyone was asking me, 'How were the English? Were they bastards?', To be honest, the English were the best and most professional on tour, the best to mix with. There was a small Irish contingent who just pissed it up, while the Scottish guys, apart from Gavin Hastings, our captain, just kept to themselves, and there were just five of us Welsh guys. Ieuan tended to keep himself to himself, but Richard Webster was very outgoing and got on with everyone, as did Robert Jones and Tony Clements, so more often than not I found myself with them in the company of all the English boys, and I enjoyed it. You do make friends for life on a trip like that. People like Jerry Guscott and Rob Andrew, for whom I still have great respect, made me feel at home, helped me grow up and made me feel a part of something special, which it was. I know we didn't win the series, but I feel I won a moral victory on that tour because I managed to avoid all the potential bad press from the taxi business (apart from the T-shirt affair, in which I was only indirectly involved) and I met a lot of nice people.

As far as Will Carling was concerned, we played together in the North Harbour game and he played in the First Test. I don't know what sort of mental state he was in, but I do know that before the match against Southland a lot of players in the squad were saying to me, 'I think you should be playing. Keep injury-free and you'll be in for the Second Test.' That was the guys telling me, not me telling myself or telling anyone else. Everyone thought Will wasn't on top of his game, but only he can answer that. He played in the First Test and I played in the second and third. It certainly didn't help that his girlfriend, Julia, was around. I know I wouldn't like that, and I know an awful lot of other players who wouldn't, because when you're on a serious tour like that girls are a distraction. Not that I ever saw him with her, but I knew she was about. And Will was a very independent, insular type of guy, so that didn't help either.

But then again he was in the spotlight all the time, which can be difficult. Everywhere we went he got all the attention, so that could have been very distracting for him as well. He was undoubtedly the highest-profile bloke on the trip. I remember one incident when someone tried to stitch him up. A girl pulled up her top right by Will and suddenly there was a camera and someone took a picture. It was obviously premeditated. Then the heavy mob took over: Dean Richards grabbed the camera and took the film out, so that was the end of that. Incidents like that can't have helped Will's state of mind, and I just took my opportunity. After Geech praised me, Will was the first guy to say, 'Well done. You deserve it. I wish you all the best.' He was very humble and very sincere.

I learned a lot about rugby on that tour, particularly from guys like Jerry Guscott, Will Carling, Rob Andrew and Gavin Hastings. I really enjoyed the way New Zealand played against us – it was my type of football. I think I could quite happily have settled and played in New Zealand. I remember reading something Buck Shelford wrote about me during the tour – 'I like the way this young boy's playing' – which was very pleasing. We didn't get any press from back home, it was just local stuff, and when I read that in one of his columns I thought, At least I've struck a note with someone who's probably worth listening to, so I reckoned I wasn't doing too bad. I actually mixed with a lot of the press, particularly Paul Rees of the *South Wales Echo*. As a player in the public eye you don't really want to get too close to the media, but I did get on well with all the journalists on tour.

I'd been out in New Zealand for nine weeks, and now I was feeling tired. The year before I hadn't had much rest, and in 1991 there was the World Cup, so I felt I'd been playing rugby virtually non-stop for ages. I simply wanted to get back home to Wales and rest.

CHAPTER FOUR

Time to Leave

I'd always been interested in rugby league. When I was growing up the Challenge Cup final was always a big thing in our house. I always remember it being a glorious day in May with a great game on show featuring people like Mick Burke of Widnes and James Leuluai from that great Hull side of the eighties. Wigan were also becoming a dominant force during this period with players like Henderson Gill and Ellery Hanley, and all those famous names just stand out for me. I can remember watching Widnes one year when Eddie Waring was commentating, and thinking, This is exciting!

As the years went by my love for league increased. The Challenge Cup was always the shop window of the sport; in fact, that's all we got to see on television. My dad explained to me why rugby league came about, why they didn't kick the ball as much as we did in rugby union, and I remember thinking, Yeah – why *do* we kick so much? Everyone ran with the ball in league, and I found I had an almost instant rapport with it.

The first offer to switch to rugby league came my way a couple of days after my second game for Wales, against Scotland in the 1991 Five Nations championship. I had a call from a scrap merchant, Dai Morris, down in Swansea who said, 'I'm a scout for Wigan. They want to sign you.' I was really surprised because at that time Dean Bell was playing in the centre for them, and they had top players like Andy Platt and Joe Lydon. I went to meet the directors in Usk, in south-east Wales, and they offered me a contract there and then. I was only just twenty at the time and had just the two caps for my country. If I'd gone for it then I'd just have been totally rugby league, and I'd probably still be there now. I would have been like some of those guys in the sixties, like Billy Boston at Wigan and Roy Mathias and John Mantle at Saints, who converted, set up house up there, married a local girl and are still there. I didn't have a problem with that, but I felt the offer came just at the wrong time for me. I'd just had a taste of international rugby union, and I hadn't really achieved anything yet.

When I came back from meeting the Wigan directors the press had picked up on it, and I think a lot of people thought, He's making it up and just trying to draw attention to himself. There were a lot of rugby league scouts and aficionados in south Wales who were a bit sceptical, and they asked me who I'd met from Wigan, expecting me not to know. So I said, 'I met Jack Hilton, Tom Rathbone, Jack Robinson and Maurice Lindsay,' the four directors of Wigan, so that kind of shut them up.

I thought that as long as I was playing well and stayed in the public eye, league clubs would be interested in signing me. At that time ex-union players Jonathan Davies, John Devereux and Paul Moriarty had all gone north and were getting on well. Sure enough, towards the end of the 1992/93 season Wigan came up with another offer, and this time I went up to Central Park in

Dai Morris's Rolls-Royce, and took my dad with me. We went into the board room and sat down and discussed things. They wanted me as a replacement for the great Australian centre Gene Miles, who was leaving at the end of the season. My dad said, 'You should do it son,' so I signed and left for home with a cheque.

I'd kept in touch with David McKnight, who'd come up with the Hull offer during the 1992 Five Nations, and when he got wind of the deal I'd signed with Wigan he rang me and said, 'I could have got you a better deal.'

I replied, 'To be honest, Dave, I didn't argue about the deal because it sounded good to me.'

Then he said, 'You know you're under contract with me, so I'm going to have to take a cut.'

He named the amount, and I told him I thought it was a bit much because he hadn't been a party in the deal and he hadn't brought it to me, even though he said he knew all the people at Wigan.

All this coincided with a documentary Martyn Williams's company Rugby Vision were doing on me, so we agreed that they would cover my last game for Swansea and then have shots of me watching the Premiership final with the cheque Wigan had given me. But then I began to have doubts, and I talked to Martyn Williams. I told him, 'I don't think I'm going to go now because it just doesn't feel right.' I rang Jack Robinson to tell him, and he said, understandably, that he was disappointed. I sent him a lovely letter saying how sorry I was, that I really wanted to do it but something inside was telling me not to. I wrote that maybe some day I'd turn out in the cherry and white of Wigan, and wished him and the club all the best. The signing-on cheque went back too.

I'd shaken hands with everyone, signed the contract, initialled all the clauses; they'd given me a signing-on fee and were setting up a press conference. It took me ages to write that letter to Jack, who seemed a lovely bloke, one of the good guys. With hindsight, I should have gone to Wigan. I would have been very raw, but I would have learnt some good habits straight away and been part of a very good side. The ironic thing was that I remember watching the Premiership final on TV at home. Ray French, the BBC commentator, said, 'This is the last we'll be seeing of Gene Miles, and there's speculation that Wigan has signed a Welsh international.'

Anyway, when I got back from the Lions tour of New Zealand my old man said that the phone hadn't stopped ringing, with all these people from rugby league wanting to talk to me. He told me that Leeds wanted to sign me, but they never rang back and nothing came of it.

I went away on holiday for a welcome break, but I was on tenterhooks. I knew I should be resting, mentally as well as physically, but all the time I was wondering whether I should profit from my success on the Lions tour and go to rugby league or carry on in union and see what happened.

By the time I got back I was in the thick of things again. Wales had a couple of early-season internationals against Japan and Canada. At that time I was still self-employed, earning myself fees for consultancy work from various people, a welcome boost to whatever I was getting from rugby plus a bit of media work. But I was seriously starting to think about turning professional. Increasingly I was thinking that I'd done everything I wanted to do in rugby union: in my first three years in the game I'd played for my country, been on a Lions tour, taken part in a World Cup and won the domestic league twice with both Neath and Swansea.

I'm always up for a challenge, and my lawyer at the time was saying that it would make perfect sense for me to switch codes now.

Then Eric Ashton, the chairman of St Helens, rang me up, and I talked to David McKnight, who said he'd been speaking to them too. Eric Hughes, who had been appointed coach, apparently wanted me, and the club seemed prepared to bend over backwards to accommodate me. We went up for a meeting. I spoke to all the people at the club and got on well with them. Jeanette Smith, the physio, checked me out and said, 'Yes, he's fine,' and Ashton assured me that they had every intention of building a good team. They were about to sign Bobbie Goulding, and already had the Samoan Apollo Perelini, Anthony Sullivan and Jonathan Griffiths, so they certainly had the makings of a good side. St Helens were a big club with a strong Welsh connection; they'd had a lot of good Welsh players in the past, so I thought, Yeah, this feels right. Wigan, their great rivals, had just signed the Saints' star centre Gary Connolly, so there was an opening for me, and St Helens seemed like the right club to go to.

We thrashed out a deal in principle, and then I went away on holiday with the boys, thinking that this was going to be my last time with them. I kept in touch with what was going on back home, and by the time I returned I was convinced I had made up my mind to play for St Helens.

At that time Anthony Clement, Robert Jones, Mike Hall, Ieuan Evans and I had set up a company to try to maximise all the boys' earning potential off the field, which we called Players Limited. The company was set up by a tax expert, Brian Williams, alongside Peter Jones, who was a lawyer with Morgan Bruce (now Morgan Co.). I asked Peter to represent me in the forthcoming St Helens deal, and he agreed. He gave me some very good impartial advice, and out of courtesy I told my fellow partners and players about the deal and asked them what they thought about it. They didn't commit themselves, but Brian Williams said, 'It sounds very good to me,' and Peter Jones added, 'It does sound like a good deal.' But despite my intentions on holiday, I still didn't know whether I should sign it, so I said to the boys, 'I'll let you know.'

It would certainly have been a good time to take the plunge. I'd have been able to take part in pre-season training and would have had a good start with them. They'd just had a good season: they'd done well in the league and beaten Wigan 10–4 in the Premiership final. I thought, If I'm going to do it, it would be better to do it at the start of the season rather than in the middle. I'd been in constant dialogue with Jonathan Davies, and he was saying, 'Scott, I can go through the pros and cons with you if you want, but why don't you just do it? We've all done it, it's a good crack. There's a good social life and everyone's great – but it's tough, mind.' I didn't have a problem with that.

But what really began to turn me off the idea were Peter Jones's words of warning. He'd had a look at the contract and started to question the viability of the club – things like: if St Helens, as a limited company, went bust, would I still get paid? He said that you could drive a bus through the contract, and it had to be tightened up. But the club said that they had the same clauses in everyone's contract. Peter did a search on St Helens and it didn't look too good, but they had been going for a hundred years and hadn't folded yet, and rugby league clubs always seem to be in strife anyway.

Then Peter said, 'Why don't we have a look at what's on offer from rugby union?' So we went to see Vernon Pugh, the chairman of the Welsh Rugby Union, and I said to him, 'I've had another offer from rugby league, which I'm seriously considering, but I'd like to know what's on the table from you first.' I wasn't giving anyone an ultimatum, I was just being honest and up front – which I was about every offer I'd had. I told him I didn't really want to leave Wales, because my family was there and I loved playing for Swansea, but I wanted a career path to work alongside my rugby and a chance to earn something. He said, 'I understand where you're coming from, but if you're asking me for eight bars of gold I can't do anything.' I told him I wasn't, and he said he'd see what he could do. I think the club and the union got together to try to work something out, because they realised there would be other players in the future who would get offers just like me, and if they wanted to keep them something had to be done.

Everyone at Swansea was bullish, saying, 'He won't go.' I showed them the figures from the rugby league deal, and said, 'If I can make something similar in rugby union, of course I'll stay.' And I meant it. I sat down again with Peter Jones and looked at what the WRU had come up with. We had a letter from them stating that this will come from here, that will come from there, and the club would endeavour to do this and that, and within three months they'd find a suitable job for me. So I decided not to sign for Saints, and I think I regretted it straight away. When I didn't sign, St Helens went straight out and bought Andy Dannatt, the prop from Hull. Eric Ashton said to me, 'If you ever change your mind, Scott, give me a call.'

I think Swansea thought it was a great coup that I wasn't going to leave. The club was now paying me a little bit indirectly from one of the guys on the board, but all in all it still wasn't working out. Several months went by, and neither the WRU or Swansea came up with anything approaching the promises made in the letter. I certainly wasn't any better off, so I rang Peter Jones to tell him I was unhappy, and he said, 'To be honest, I don't think it's working out either. Shall I try to resurrect the deal with St Helens?' But when we spoke to Eric Ashton, he said, 'We haven't got enough money to do anything now, but leave it and we'll come back to you. We'll look to sort out something before the Challenge Cup deadline.' Eric had always been very up front and honest with me, so that gave me a bit of hope.

In December 1993 I played for the Barbarians against New Zealand. I was also due to be a guest on *A Question of Sport* on the Sunday, and I thought, Great! I've cracked it now, I'm really going places. I thought that if I had a good game for the Barbarians, hopefully Saints would be encouraged to sign me before the deadline in early January 1994, which would make me eligible to play in the Challenge Cup. We were playing New Zealand at Cardiff Arms Park, and it was my second Barbarians outing. Ian McGeechan was coach, and at half-time I was complaining about a backache and was thinking about going off, but I decided to battle on as things were going all right for me. Then Jeff Wilson, the New Zealand wing, jumped on me and my leg buckled. It ended up at right angles to my foot, and I was in agony.

It seemed like every time good news was on the horizon something bad happened, and this was a serious injury. As soon as I came off the field I knew I was knackered. When I got to the medical room the foot felt a little better, so I put some weight on it, but it gave way. The left lateral ligament had come off the bone completely, and I'd torn the hamstring, the calf muscles and the membrane from behind the knee, the meniscus. Only the anterior cruciate ligament was left intact, which was miraculous; all the physios who had seen a still of my leg assumed it had gone because my knee was in total hyperextension. I underwent surgery within forty-eight hours.

The injury was badly timed in a few other ways. Tony

Underwood and I had had a bet on the Lions tour that we'd both learn the saxophone by the New Year. It transpired that the BBC had picked up on it, so Tony had come to Cardiff and we'd had a practice session in front of the cameras. They were going to follow it up on the Saturday night after the Barbarians game. I'd learned my piece, he'd learned his, and we were going to play as a trio with another guy. It was going to be such a good weekend, but it all fell through thanks to the injury. I was also due to go skiing the week after, so that obviously wasn't going to happen now. I began to regret not coming off at half-time with backache; after all, it was only a Barbarians game, and Christian Scholtz from South Africa, who came on for me at the end, had been itching to get on. I should have given him a crack at it earlier on. I missed out on *A Question of Sport* too.

I thought at one point that there was a chance I wouldn't play again. You always think things like that when you get a bad injury. Ian McGeechan sent a card to the hospital with a nicely worded note in it, which buoyed me up a bit. Mike Ruddock, the Swansea coach, came to see me, and I took calls from Will Carling and Gavin Hastings. Eric Ashton also called to say, 'Don't worry, lad, just get fit and we'll have another look at you.' I thought, If he can ring me and the Welsh Rugby Union can't, then there's something wrong here. Apart from Mike Ruddock and one or two others, I didn't have a lot of support, and I began to see people in their true colours. I think the view from the WRU was, Oh, he's injured – we'll just get someone else.

The sponsors of the Barbarians were the insurance company Scottish Amicable, but that didn't do me much good because I ended up £1,500 out of pocket. The bill for the MRI scan (like an X-ray, but magnetic resonance imaging shows up more detail) came and I paid for that; I also had to pay for all my physiotherapy because I didn't think I was doing the right exercises originally. No one from the Barbarians came to see me in hospital when I was in plaster, and I became so disillusioned with it all. There was insurance, but it didn't do me any good. Luckily, I went to see Tim Atter from BUPA in Cardiff, and he got me on the right track by allowing me to use their facilities at a concessionary rate, but I still had to pay. Admittedly at that time Swansea were still paying me, but I didn't have any help or encouragement from the WRU. I was just left alone, so I thought, Sod it!

I was in plaster for six weeks over the Christmas and New Year period, and then it was all down to constant rehab. I started going to Bridgend Hospital to see a physiotherapist friend of mine, Nicky Munson, and gradually began to cycle. I remembered Eric Ashton's words and had no doubt in my mind that as soon as I was fit again I'd sign for Saints. I also decided that I wasn't going to tell anyone about my plans, especially at Swansea. All the time I'd been honest with them, and I was only asking for some help to continue my union career. Whether they tried, or just didn't try hard enough, I don't know, but I thought this time I'm not going to bother talking to them because they'd dissuaded me every other time. I didn't play for Swansea again.

Come April, I asked Dave McKnight if Saints were still looking, and he told me they were still interested and he would put something together. Of course the deal wasn't as good as it was before because I was damaged goods, but I was hell-bent on going, and as soon as things were sewn up I was so relieved because I knew then it was the right time. From that time on I just focused on getting fit and signing for St Helens later that season. Richard Webster had had enough too. He signed for Salford, and I remember saying to him, 'I'll be with you soon.'

At that time I had an opportunity to learn a different business with a company called Microsystems, but the timing of it was poor because of my injury and subsequent deal with St Helens. Of course, I should have had the courtesy to ring in and say I wouldn't be going, but at the time I didn't want to talk to anyone who might try to dissuade me and say I was doing the wrong thing. I was absolutely determined that this time I would make my own decision and stick to it.

I signed for St Helens in April 1994, and they told me to come back in July. I knew there'd be a lot of animosity and bad press back home, so me and a mate of mine just took off for a couple of weeks. I knew there would be fellow players slagging me off (and they did), and certainly no one at Swansea approved of what I'd done or the way I'd gone about it, and I can understand their attitude. There wasn't the same animosity surrounding Richard Webster's move, or Jonathan Davies's or Paul Moriarty's for that matter. I suppose it was because the drama of my 'defection' had been drawn out over two or three years. Because of the time that had elapsed, everyone thought that Swansea and the Welsh Rugby Union had bent over backwards to sort me out so I could stay in rugby union, and I'd still snubbed them. The press played up to this; it was heavily publicised, for instance, that I'd lost my licence and Swansea had got me a chauffeur and an apartment in Swansea. In fact, the driver was just one of the boys, and I had the use of an apartment in Swansea belonging to one of the directors because I lived forty minutes away in Pencoed and it didn't make sense for me to commute for training and matches. But everyone was thinking, Look at him, he's got everything – but in reality that was far from the truth.

Swansea thought I'd be fit by the summer and be back playing with them for the 1994/95 season, so my decision to leave came right out of the blue. Of course the first thing the press did was to ring the club, and their initial reaction was that they were pissed off. Mike James, the Swansea chairman, called me a rugby prostitute. I rang him straight away and asked him why he thought it was necessary to call me that. He told me that as chairman of the club he had to be seen to say the right things, and officially that was the view of everyone at Swansea. 'Personally,' he said, 'I think you've made the right decision.' If I'd done it in an amicable way and said to them, 'It isn't working out, I'm joining St Helens,' everyone would have been a lot happier because at least I'd have been totally honest with them, but I was still feeling bitter and twisted from the fact that no one from the WRU had had the decency to ring me up or send me a card when I was injured. Even when I turned up at training at Swansea while I was still recuperating I was kind of shunned because I was useless. I might not have been honest with them, but at least I was being honest with myself. Going to rugby league was what I'd wanted to do for the last couple of years, yet everyone had dissuaded me from doing it. They all said it was the wrong move, but no one had come up and offered me a proper viable alternative. None of what they promised me came to fruition.

When I got back from holiday I began commuting by train from south Wales to St Helens; I'd go up during the week and come back at weekends to get all my stuff. One day, when I was walking over the crossing in Pencoed on my way up to my dad's house, some guy in a van shouted, 'Why don't you fuck off where you belong – up north!' I thought, Well, that just about sums it all up. Feelings like that had been brewing over the years. Wales is reputed to be such a friendly place, but it's no better than anywhere else. I had a far better welcome in St Helens when I joined, and I still have good friends up there. The comment from that guy just typified the old Welsh mentality: they'd rather see everyone have nothing than someone have something. Yet this was the place I was born and brought up in. The following year, when a lot of the Welsh boys came back for the rugby league World Cup, we were treated like kings and there was a totally different vibe about it. But when I left it certainly wasn't like that.

CHAPTER FIVE

A Different League

I went up to St Helens for pre-season training in the summer of 1994, and because I didn't have a car, I had to get there by train from Bridgend to Runcorn. Anthony Sullivan, the Saints winger, was great; he picked me up and took me over to St Helens. I usually went home at the weekends, but during the week I'd stay at the Griffin Inn in Eccleston, a couple of miles from the ground. I was there for about a fortnight before Malcolm Kay, one of the club directors, took me round to see a couple of houses.

Of course I hadn't played rugby since December 1993, and my concern since then had been to get my knee as strong as possible. I'd done a lot of strength work but wasn't able to do any cardiovascular stuff, so I knew my first training session was going to be tough. In fact, I always found the training tough in rugby league. We just ran and ran and ran, and when I thought we couldn't run any more we'd tuck into another forty minutes of running. It was very much like being back at Neath. We'd start off with an hour and a half of skills, which wasn't a problem, but I was shocked that some of the boys didn't seem to have good ball skills. We did a lot of interval runs and track work, which I struggled with for the best part of that season. We trained very hard that year, but I just couldn't get to grips with it. I still had some scar tissue from my knee injury and didn't manage to complete some of the track sessions, so those who had turned up to watch began to mutter, 'He doesn't look very fast.'

I'd had a full medical before signing and was all in one piece, I just wasn't fit after six months out. To be honest, I didn't really know how tough the training was going to be. I thought a lot of the guys would be bigger than they were, but everyone was very lean. In that first training session we did a couple of sprints and all the props beat me. There were little things I had to learn, like being square at play-the-balls – i.e. standing in front of the man who's just been tackled. I and Apollo Perelini had a couple of sessions with Eric Hughes on playing the ball, and we went through a couple of basis plays, and I soon got to grips with the terminology.

Anthony Sullivan was the first squad member I met, when he picked me up from the station, but at that first training session I met all the other players. Allan Hunte came over and said, 'Very nice to see you,' in his best northern accent. The rest of them seemed a bit stand-offish, as though they were waiting to make up their minds. They were probably looking at me thinking, 'Who the hell's this guy?'

We'd train twice a week as well as Saturday morning. I was excused from the Saturday morning session if I wanted to go home. We all had to do weight training, which I was happy with, but I was shocked to see that a lot of them hadn't really been in a gym. They didn't know what they were doing, apart from me and Anthony Sullivan, so we bonded a bit more because I knew my way around a gym. Gym work was fine, it was just the running that was a problem. Whenever I thought it was all over and I was on my hands and knees spewing, we'd do more. I'd never seen so many people run that far.

I played my first game in a friendly against Widnes, coming on at half-time. I scored a couple of tries and it seemed to go well. I didn't mind being thrown in at the deep end; I wanted to get stuck in straight away. For one thing I wanted to test my knee to the maximum, so when I played against Widnes every time I had the ball I picked the biggest bastard on their side, who just happened to be a Tongan prop called Lee Hansen, and ran at him. After the game the boys said, 'Gibbsy, don't run at the big guys, especially not the likes of Lee Hansen,' but I didn't have a problem with it. I didn't get hurt. However, the first time I touched the ball in the match I dropped it, for two reasons: one, I was nervous on my debut; and two, one of the Hulme brothers said, 'You fucking Welsh bastard, why don't you fuck off home?' That was the first time I came across 'trash talking', which happened a lot. After that initial experience I didn't have a problem with it. I realised very early on that you have to give as good as you get in rugby league, otherwise you get picked on, and that's why Hansen and all these people were running at me. They were testing me because, being new, I was potentially a weak link.

We didn't have a great start to our league campaign that season. Our first match was against Doncaster, who had just been promoted, and they ended up beating us. Vila Matautia, who later came to Saints, was playing, and so was the South African Jamie Bloem, who, being a true Bokker, was having a go at Allan Hunte and Sully. At the final whistle all the crowd started booing us. I couldn't understand it; I'd never experienced that in my life before. But I thought I'd done all right, and the reports in the papers were quite kind to me early on because Allan was scoring and I was putting him in and doing my fair share of the work. I wasn't averse to working hard or taking the ball into contact situations – I thought it was the norm. I quickly found out that some of the players didn't like working too much.

That first week was very difficult, because after losing to Doncaster we were away the following Wednesday evening at Warrington. I was still sore from Sunday's exertions on the morning of the match, and when the time came to jump on the bus, I thought, Christ, can this get any worse? Yes, because Warrington kicked off straight to me. I think Saints were the only side at that time that had their centres on the ten-metre line – most sides had props and second rows to take the first drive. So when Warrington kicked off to me, I caught the ball and, throwing caution to the wind, ran full pelt, jumped up in the air with my elbows out and got dumped by Paul Cullen, Mark Hilton and Bruce McGuire. I found myself on the floor, making all these moaning noises, and I could hear Jiffy (Jonathan Davies) laughing his head off in his squeaky little way. I ran into Mark Hilton, the Warrington prop, once again later on and I was in cloud-cuckoo-land for ten minutes. I learnt early on that it was indeed sensible not to run into the big boys – far better to run into the middle of the field where the half-backs and smaller players were. But of course when you get the ball you haven't got a lot of time to make a decision, so I just used to pick the straightest route, and more often than not it led to the biggest guys.

I was quite pleased with the first couple of games I played, though my knowledge of the game wasn't that great yet. But I took everything in and I didn't have a problem with what they wanted me to do, proving to everyone that I wasn't a dumb footballer. I was still a little unsure of the rules, though; when the ball was kicked over our own try line, for instance, I didn't know what to do. On one occasion I was in two minds, so I just grabbed it and touched it down, whereas I should have thrown it out of play or tried to play it.

I also had to come to grips with the differences in playing centre in union and league. Eric Hughes, the Saints coach, had been a centre, and Paul Loughlin, one of the club's current centres, quickly befriended me, as did Phil Veivers, the St Helens full-back, so I had a lot of good people around me, and their best advice was, 'Follow the ball and stay in the line.' I quickly got a grasp on the game and learned all the plays, which was a shock to most people, particularly Eric Ashton and Eric Hughes. I took to it like a duck to water, as if I'd been playing all my life, because I found it simple to play. I had no problem coping with the logistics of the sport. Whether I was a good player or not is for other people to say, but I was consistent and played a lot of games on the trot – and, of course, got bruised and battered on a regular basis.

The Sunday after the midweek Warrington game we were away to Halifax, and I thought, Jesus, it doesn't get any easier. When we got there the pitch was on a slope and the changing rooms were awful. Of course, as the new kid on the block I had the worst seat in the place. They put me right in the corner; I couldn't lift my head up without hitting the ceiling. At the start of the game they kicked off to me, and the next thing I knew I was running into Karl Harrison, the Great Britain prop, and their other big second row, Paul Round, so I got smashed up again. But I remember making a burst and going through Gary Divorty before flicking the ball to Allan. He scored, and we ended up winning. That was the first time anyone said, 'Well done, Scott.' At that time I didn't know how much winning money meant to a lot of the boys.

My contract at St Helens was for four years. I received a basic salary, and on top of that there was always a matchplay bonus. A home win netted about £350, and for away wins it was a bit more – about £400 – because it was tougher. If we drew away from home we'd also get winning money. There was an appendix to the contract saying that bonuses for cup games would be negotiated with senior players at the club, and a fines system operated, based on club rules. I think we got about £75 for losing, too, and of course tax was taken out of that.

After six games I noticed that I was coping better in training, and my physique had changed completely, but I'd never been so fatigued after matches in my whole career. It was very, very tough. Even now, when I meet anyone who plays rugby league at any level, I have the utmost respect for them. The players deserve all the rewards they get and more, because it's such a wonderful, demanding sport. You'll never hear me say a bad word about the game. I love it.

For the first six months I was living on my own, but I settled in quite happily. I remember Mally Kay, one of the directors, telling me that some of the boys didn't drink, and I recalled that when I went to Wigan Jack Robinson had told me that some of their players, like Martin Offiah, were teetotallers. After my first games for Saints I almost understood why: if you always felt as shattered as this after eighty minutes, it's no wonder you don't feel like a drink. When I first got there after the training sessions the boys would head straight for the Pilkington club at Ruskin Drive where each would have about eight pints of Guinness. They would ask me how hard rugby union was, and I'd tell them it was a piece of cake compared to this training. They also asked, 'Do rugby union boys drink a lot?' and I replied, 'Not really. Only on a Saturday night.' So I quickly found out that not all rugby league boys were teetotal, and I was in good company with Phil Veivers, Paul

Loughlin and the others. Jon Neill, the prop, had a stag night early on, so I was invited to that and got to meet all the boys socially. As I said, they were a bit stand-offish at first, but it didn't take long for them to come round. I soon found myself going out more often than I should. Paul Loughlin had a testimonial dinner in those early weeks, and when he stood up his first words were to welcome me to the club. He didn't have to say that, but it was something from the heart, and I struck up a friendship with him and Phil Veivers for the rest of my time there.

When the season really got under way it became impossible to go back to south Wales at the weekend. I was really enjoying my rugby, although it was still painful after games. The boys would just say, 'You'll get used to it,' but I don't know if you ever really get used to it. I couldn't walk up and down the stairs after a game; every part of my body would ache: my thumbs, my cheekbones, my earlobes. When my girlfriend Sharyn came up and I was driving again, I would leave the club straight away after a game, go back to the house, have some food and go to bed. I was just so knackered.

When I first played against Wigan, on Boxing Day at Knowsley Road, my dad and a whole load of people from south Wales came up, and they stayed in a hotel by the Haydock Park racecourse. We had dinner together after the game, but then I said I had to go home because I was so shattered. I just needed to go to bed. The derby matches against Wigan were played hard and fast at what seemed like a million miles per hour. That was a step up for me, because there was a massive crowd and a lot of tension. We lost, but it was a great experience, and I can see why there is that rivalry because everyone talks about it. You can just hear the disappointment in the crowd, because all the spectators desperately want you to beat Wigan.

Towards the end of the year I'd also got to play against Australia. They were on tour, and after playing against them for Wales on Sunday, 30 October, I ended up facing them for a second time in a St Helens shirt at Knowsley Road the following Tuesday. It was a massive game in front of a big crowd, and we didn't back down that night. Players like Jon Neill and Sonny Nickle really gave it to their big forwards, and at half-time we were leading. In the end their big guns started firing and we ended up losing 32–14, but it was a great evening.

The club had had a poor start to the season, but we gradually managed to get a few good results under our belt. By December, when the Regal Trophy competition came round, and then the Challenge Cup in January, I was really enjoying myself. We lost narrowly, 24–22, to Wigan in the quarter-final of the Regal Trophy, then drew them in the first round proper of the Challenge Cup. We had a fantastic match at Central Park which ended in a 16–16 draw, but in the replay at Knowsley Road on 12 February 1995 we were hammered 40–24 and I ended up dislocating my elbow and missing the rest of the season. I was quite happy with the way things had gone, but it had all seemed to go so quickly.

Allan Hunte and I had met up with Bobby Fulton, the coach to the Manly club, when he was over here with the Australian team, and he had invited us both to play for Manly during the summer of 1995. Allan didn't go for some reason, and I thought the elbow injury had put paid to me going out there, but then Fulton rang me and said, 'Why don't you come out for a couple of weeks anyway? If you're not fit to play just take it as a holiday.' So Sharyn and I went over at the end of May, and we had a great time. They wanted to have a good look at my elbow, so I had a scan and the doctor said, 'You should be playing by now.' It had been sixteen weeks since the dislocation, and he said I should have been back after six, but because it was towards the end of the season and St Helens were out of both cup competitions, and out of contention in the league, there hadn't been a big rush to get me fit.

I'd met most of the Manly players before, and I had a couple of beers with them. They took us down to the harbour on our first day there and everyone was great. Bob Fulton asked if Sharyn wanted to go on the water, but I said that she didn't like sailing, so he said, 'Well, my daughter's going shopping this afternoon, so she can either go with her or stay in the house with my wife.' They couldn't do enough for us. Sharyn ended up on the beach reading while I went out and had a good time with the Manly boys. Then I met up with Cliffie Lyons, the Manly half-back, to whom Jonathan Davies had introduced me on the tour with Wales in 1991.

They all reckoned my elbow was in good nick, and that they could get me fit. We'd only been there a couple of days when I did a session with their fitness guy, who wanted to assess me. He said I was some way off the level of Cliffie Lyons and their scrum-half Geoff Toovey, but I was probably only two weeks or so off playing. That wasn't bad considering I'd been inactive for about four months and couldn't do a lot as my arm was in a sling.

So the next thing the fitness guy said was, 'Right, Scott, we'll pick you up in the morning.'

I said, 'Right. What time?'

'Ten to five.'

So the next morning, bright and early, Brian Hollis, the club's trainer, took me to a gym in east Sydney and gave me a good workout. Then we went round the corner to have breakfast before he dropped me off at Darling Harbour, where I caught the ferry back home to Manly. I did that a few times.

Everyone at Manly was very professional; they were like the

Manchester United of rugby league. At their home ground, Brookvale Oval, each player had his own locker and his own drink in the fridge. They had use of a great gym, and in the clubhouse they had ballrooms and a Chinese restaurant. It was all very impressive.

I watched Manly play Brisbane, and it was nearly an hour before anyone missed a tackle. It was incredible. Then we flew down to Melbourne to watch a State of Origin match – one of a series of games between Queensland and New South Wales featuring players born in those states – but Sharyn and I missed the game because we were still jet-lagged. After a good sleep we met up with Dave McKnight, who had just come over from New Zealand where he had closed the deal to take Denis Betts from Wigan to the Auckland Warriors. We went out for dinner, and I got the distinct impression everything was getting a bit too serious.

When we went back to Manly they were talking about when I was going to play, and I felt the pressure building. I told them I had to get back to St Helens in plenty of time for pre-season training in July, and then they turned up the heat. I rang Frank Stanton, the chief executive of Manly, and said, 'Look, we've got to get back. Summer camp is starting in a few weeks and I don't want to be late. Eric Ashton's probably going to be on the phone to give me a hard time.' He said, 'Don't go back, stay with us.' I told him I wasn't fit to play, but he insisted that it didn't matter. I said I couldn't break my contract, but he didn't seem to think the contract was a problem. He said, 'Don't worry about that, we'll face that when we come to it.' And in my other ear I heard Dave McKnight saying, 'It sounds good. If I never do business with St Helens ever again, so what?' Stanton then offered me a king's ransom not to go back to England, but I'd only just started with Saints, I'd just bought a house and a car, we had cats to look after, and I just couldn't stay in Australia and delegate all responsibility to my dad. I told Frank that being away from my family in Wales was bad enough, but going off to Australia was something else. It was gorgeous out there, and the facilities were amazing, but I said no.

I think we made a mistake in coming back so promptly, but I panicked a bit. At that time the Super League/ARL war was raging and money was being thrown at players. All the Great Britain internationals were signing for one or the other, but because I was locked into a long-term agreement with St Helens, it wasn't going to do anyone any good to sign me. Manly at the time were ARL, and their asking me to stay was all a bit too good to be true. All the wheeling and dealing was a bit much for us, whereas it all seemed so natural to them. They did everything to accommodate me. They had it in their heads that I was going to play for them in a couple of weeks. I don't think there was a hidden agenda when they invited me out there, but they obviously liked what they saw. I had played rugby league for just one season but I must have made an impression on Bobby Fulton, because when I was doing some work with their fitness guy, Matthew Ridge, their New Zealand international full-back, said, 'Who's this guy? He doesn't look like a rugby player,' but Bob came right back with, 'Don't worry, Ridgey. This guy can play.'

When we got on the plane to go home, I did wonder whether I'd made the right choice. The timing of my injuries has often played a crucial role in terms of my future – whether that's fate or not, I don't know. I would have loved to stay in Australia, though.

At that time we were still playing in the old Stones Bitter First Division, but just before I left for Australia the Super League was being put into place. The World Cup was also happening that autumn, and I was quite excited about turning out for Wales. But the lure of Manly was strong. I rang Bob Fulton when I got back to England, and he said, 'Don't worry, we'll have a chat after the World Cup and do something after that.' But after the World Cup I left messages in his hotel and rang him when he got home, but I didn't get to speak to him. The next thing I knew the Leeds centre Craig Innes had signed for Manly. I put two and two together and reasoned that I was still locked into a contract with St Helens, whereas Craig Innes was in his last year at Leeds, so it was easier for Dave McKnight to shift him than me. It wasn't a major problem for me, but I certainly saw it like it was: a missed opportunity.

CHAPTER SIX

Marching in with the Saints

When I got back from Australia, English rugby league clubs were looking at two seasons in one, because there was to be a shortened Stones Bitter Centenary Championship starting in August 1995 and finishing in January 1996, and then the new Super League would kick off in March.

I came back to summer camp and coped with the training schedule a lot better than the previous year. I was looking forward to the new season because I no longer felt as though I was under the microscope. Tommy Martyn had been injured in one of the last games of the previous season and needed major surgery on his knee, so the club was struggling to find a stand-off. Eric Hughes talked to me about playing there for the early part of the season as it would be a while before they could get Karle Hammond, signed from Widnes but having a stint in Sydney before joining Saints. It made me think that I must be doing something right after just a short time in the game if they wanted me to play stand-off.

I played a pre-season game against Salford in the position and thought, Jesus, this is different. You're so much more involved in the play and have to do a lot more defensive work, and you've got to organise things a bit more. The weather was really hot at the start of the season, but we kicked off with a very good win against Bradford at Knowsley Road, 55–10, and then we beat Oldham 44–18 and I scored a couple of tries. But we lost heavily to Wigan, 52–20, and then went down 36–24 at Leeds in a game we could have won but didn't because we spilled too much ball.

After that Leeds defeat Eric Hughes came into the dressing room, as usual, and really lost his head. He'd take his teeth out for moments like this and start screaming and shouting, effing and blinding. He ended, 'I'll speak to you in the morning. I want everyone in early.' So we all turned up on Monday morning, and he said, 'I'll teach you to respect that ball. We're going to train all day, every day this week.' He went on, 'All you lot are worried about is mobile phones, golf, shagging, drinking and Ford Probes. You're a bunch of fucking playboys.' It was lashing down with rain at the time and we all wondered what the hell was going on. Eric then proceeded to run us into the ground, although I think we stopped for a short rest at lunchtime. Every time we spilled the ball he made us pay for it. After that first day our morale was at rock-bottom. We were still feeling knackered after the Sunday game and he'd really hammered us in training. I didn't think it was the way to go about it, but he was trying to make a point, I suppose.

On Tuesday it was the same again, and we all thought, Christ, he can't go on like this! But we went through Wednesday and Thursday in identical fashion, and then Eric came round a bit and began to laugh it all off, saying, 'Well, I think you've all learned your lesson now.' Our next game was up at Workington, and we went straight back to our winning ways. I scored a good try in that

66–22 victory, and then we beat Sheffield 62–20 at home. We were right back on track.

Around this time the Australian coach Shaun McRae was in the country conducting some training seminars. He came to Saints for a week and we trained up at the Liverpool St Helens rugby union ground. He knew a lot of drills, and, to be honest, this was probably the first time I became stimulated by rugby league training because he was offering us something different. I think he did sessions with a couple of clubs over here and was very highly thought of. He had been an assistant coach with the Canberra Raiders and had done a lot of work at the Australian Institute of Sport. A lot of the conditioning stuff he was doing was very interesting. It was a different week for us, a different voice, and I enjoyed it.

The World Cup was the big event that year, so in October I was deeply involved in the preparations of the Welsh squad. Everyone who was part of that squad still speaks about it, because it was a brilliant month. I knew all the ex-rugby union players of course, but some of the other guys I didn't know so well, people like Iestyn Harris, who had a great World Cup. Clive Griffiths was the coach and Mike Nicholas the manager, and it was a fun time to be around. There was a good buzz about the tournament back in Wales, even though I don't think the competition was marketed very well there, if at all. Nobody seemed to know there was a game on, but it soon clicked when they saw us around. All the prodigal sons were returning home, and we made the most of it and drew the maximum out of the crowd. We had a fabulous welcome everywhere – in particular from restaurateurs, who'd just open their arms and invite us in – maybe because people realised that for a lot of the high-profile guys, like Jonathan Davies, this was their swan song. Rugby union in Wales was still in turmoil, too, and not really going anywhere, so we were an attraction. I really felt at home for the first time in a long while, and comfortable in the red jersey.

We really looked the part, too. The squad trained hard, and we opened the tournament with a 28–6 win against France, but I missed the next game, against Western Samoa, because I'd injured my knee and needed a week to get it right. I would have been up against great players like Va'aiga Tuigamala and Tea Ropati, so I was really pissed off, but I knew I couldn't play because I could hardly walk. But I remember the game at the Vetch in Swansea vividly; it was one of the most brutal rugby league encounters I've ever witnessed in these waters. It was so exciting. I sat next to Phil Ford in the stand and we went through two packets of extra strong mints between us. The game was absolutely compelling. There must have been 16,000 at the Vetch and it was an historic night. When people look back at great sporting occasions at the Vetch, harking back to the days when Swansea City were in the First Division, that rugby league match will be right up there. Wales won it 22–10, and I really wished I could have been on the field that night. It was very, very physical, but we didn't back off; people like Paul Moriarty and David Young tackled like demons and ran hard. It was brilliant. We celebrated after that, as you can imagine.

We also qualified fairly comfortably for the semis as winners of our group, along with England, New Zealand and Australia. We went up to Manchester to train ahead of our match with England at Old Trafford. There was another massive crowd at Old Trafford, and it was a great occasion. I remember Martin Offiah scoring a couple of times in the corner, but the Samoa game had taken so much out of the Welsh forwards. The likes of Kelvin Skerrett, Martin Hall, Neil Cowie, Dai Young and Paul Moriarty, our biggest guys, were shattered, but they kept taking it up and getting smashed. We just didn't have enough cover to make an impact against England. When you looked at their group, okay, they had played Australia first up, but then they had Fiji, who they hammered 46–0, and South Africa, who they beat easily with the same scoreline. So their big match was two matches ago, but ours had been just six days earlier. That really took its toll, and England won 25–10, but we didn't gripe about it because we knew that if we'd been fresh we could have given them a tougher game, and maybe made the final. It was a good Welsh team and there was a lot of competition for places. I have great memories of that month.

I went back to St Helens after Wales's exit from the tournament, but my knee was still playing up and I missed a few games. We had some good wins, but when it came to the game against our nemesis Wigan at Central Park on Boxing Day we fielded a weakened side. We were due to play Warrington in the Regal Trophy semi-final a week later, and I remember Eric Hughes saying, 'Right, let's just try and win some silverware, shall we?' A lot of the guys were injured, and there was flu in the camp as well, so he said, 'If anyone asks, we've all gone down with the flu.' It was snowing on Christmas Day that year, and Sharyn and I had run out of eggs at the house, so we travelled over to Rainford and borrowed a couple from one of the pubs there. By the time we came back it was snowing heavily, and I doubted whether the match would start at all on Boxing Day, but it did, and we were blown away 58–4.

The other reason Eric had fielded a weakened side against Wigan was that St Helens were just about to play three games in the space of about eight days. We played Leeds at home on New Year's Day 1996 and lost 20–14. I scored one and had one disallowed, but we should have won that game. When it came to the Regal Trophy semi-final a few days later we gave Warrington a real battering, notching up eighty points without reply. It was one of those games where everything just went right. All the plays we'd practised came off, and we were breaking tackles all over the place. Bobbie Goulding was on song that day, and when things are going well for him he's unbelievable.

Incredibly, our next game was just three days later, against Warrington again, so we had to pick ourselves up yet again for that. I remember Iestyn Harris trying so hard to break through the Saints' line, but by then I'd worked out when he was going to step by reading his body language, and every time he tried it we snuffed him out. We had another good win against them, 54–14, which set us up very nicely for the Regal Trophy final against – you guessed it – Wigan.

It was the first time a final had been played at the McAlpine Stadium in Huddersfield, and it was a really impressive venue. We were definitely in with a shout of beating Wigan and taking the trophy. We felt comfortable in the early part of the game; we were defending well and running the ball well, and had some good plays. But at one stage in the first half the ball was chipped through and I went back to gather it. I tried to force the ball back in play, but I lost it, and Tuigamala scored. We were disappointed, but by no means out of the game. It was just a case of saying, 'We've given away a soft try, but we must get back up there.' And we did claw our way back into it. We scored a couple of great tries through Joey Hayes and Paul Newlove to lead at half-time, but late in the game, when we were trying to get away from our own line, I took the ball up and stuck my elbow in someone's face, which resulted in me being sent off. I thought it was a harsh decision, especially because the game was nearly over anyway. We lost that final in the end by nine points, 25–16, and I was a bit more dejected than the other guys because of the sending-off. The match was live on BBC television, and it was the first time I'd ever been dismissed. I can't remember even being sin-binned before that, so it was a real shock to the system.

That defeat signalled the end of Eric Hughes's reign as coach. The following week I turned up at Knowsley Road to face the London Broncos, and found all the boys sitting down with long faces. I asked what was up, and they said, 'Eric's got the sack.' It was a bit of a shock because there'd been no hints or rumours of anything like that happening. Maybe the results weren't good enough or there was a lack of confidence in him – I don't really know the reason for his dismissal. Being my usual self I just said, 'Right, we've got a game on. The quicker we get the game over, the quicker I can get home.' We kicked off, the Broncos went the length of the field and nearly scored, and I thought, 'Right, we're either in for a hard night or an easy night.' As it turned out we won 48–18.

I got on well with Eric Hughes. He gave me a lot of advice, and I thought he was a great guy. Coaching-wise, I wasn't in a position to criticise because I was new to the game and hadn't played at his level, so it wasn't for me to say whether he was a good rugby league coach or not. He seemed to be slowly building a good side, so I don't know why he was sacked at all. I certainly didn't have any problems with him, and I think being shown the door came as a shock to him as well. Maybe some of the players had gone back to the board and said, 'Hey, we really enjoyed the week we had with Shaun McRae, it was very worthwhile,' and that put ideas into their heads. Maybe some of the players just weren't happy with Eric. Whatever happened, I and the rest of the players now had to build a rapport with a new coach.

We had just one more championship match left, at Halifax, where we again fielded a weakened side and got beaten 32–24, to finish fourth in the championship. Suddenly the shortened season was over and we were preparing for the first ever Super League season.

The first time I remember hearing about the Super League was roughly April 1995 when I picked up a copy of *The Times* and there was a big exposé on it, but I thought it was just another rumour. Then I was told that Sky were putting the money up and it was definitely going to happen, and it did. We were all excited because we thought, Great, summer rugby! We don't have to play in the cold and rain up in Doncaster and places like that. It's going to be a lot better! There were a lot of sceptics, but I think it was definitely the way to go and I think rugby union, too, would be better suited to faster grounds in the summer.

Super League did the deal with the Rugby Football League over here, but it wasn't so clear-cut in Australia. The Australian Rugby League wanted to keep control of the competition and there was a split, with some clubs going over to Super League and others staying loyal to the ARL. Because Super League had signed up a lot of the big-name Australians to play in their competition, the ARL came over to England and tried to sign up some British players to play in theirs. Jonathan Davies signed for them, and Kevin Ellis did the same. Kevin just happened to be with Jonathan in the car when he went to the hotel to meet the ARL people, so he left the hotel with a deal as well! I didn't get too excited because I wasn't a Great Britain international, and they were the main targets, and I was only just over a year into my four-year contract with St Helens at the time. The ARL were only interested in trying to poach players who were coming out of their contracts, because it was easier. But there was a lot of general excitement and a lot of talk in the gym. All the Great Britain internationals at the club were saying, 'Have you heard anything?' Anthony Sullivan was even ringing me up and asking if I knew anything.

Then the Super League people came to me. I don't really know why, because I'd done nothing to earn it, but they gave me a cheque. All I had to do was commit myself to another couple of years or so, and when I weighed everything up it seemed worth it. But I had to pay them back if I decided to go back to rugby union, which effectively limited my future career option; it was something I was taking with one hand, but potentially giving back with the other. I felt I mightn't benefit in the long term, but everyone else was so excited. There was money flying everywhere. Some players must have missed the boat, but a lot benefited.

Of course Super League meant that everyone would now be full-time professionals. When I started at St Helens I assumed everyone there was going to be full-time, but they weren't; training was on Tuesday and Thursday evenings and Saturday mornings, so it was very much as it was back home in my union days. As soon as Super League started, we said, 'Why don't we train in the afternoons now we're all available?' So we started training during the day, but it all got a bit out of hand. We would find ourselves training on Monday morning, Monday afternoon, Tuesday morning, Tuesday afternoon, etc. It was only when Shaun McRae was appointed as the new St Helens coach that a bit of discipline in this respect was imposed, and things were managed much better. I remember the club was looking to speak to one of the coaches at Manchester United just to see how the players there coped with a professional set-up and managed their training time. The last thing they wanted was for people to see the St Helens boys walking round and hanging around betting offices, or playing snooker in the afternoon. That wouldn't have gone down too well with the supporters.

I learned a lot of good habits under McRae while I was up there in terms of self-discipline, time-keeping and attitude to training.

The players were very professional and very efficient, and their application to training was very good, far better than most rugby union players, although that's slowly improving. When Shaun McRae came things started to get a bit more meticulous. Each of us had an information folder and sat down on Monday mornings to talk about the week: how it would be planned, when our rest periods were, when we were training, whatever. It was good. He offered us incentives, things like, 'If you train well today, I'll give you tomorrow off,' so it kept everyone very buoyant.

He also brought in video analysis. I know a lot of players hate that kind of analytical work – we do it now at Swansea, and it's boring – but Shaun McRae had the process honed perfectly: it would last ten minutes and no more. He would just concentrate on key players and key moves, which is really all you need to know, rather than just ploughing through tape after tape for hours on end. He certainly had his finger on the pulse.

It was very refreshing to have a new coach because there was a different approach to everything. We'd play on the Sunday and then have a rest on the Monday. When Eric Hughes was there, it was very much the old way of doing things. After a match on Sunday, a lot of players would probably have a couple of beers on the Monday, turn up for treatment at about five o'clock in the afternoon, then go out on Monday night. But as soon as Shaun came, he instilled better habits. We'd be in the swimming pool on Monday morning and we'd work hard, doing about twenty lengths; then he'd leave it up to us in the afternoon whether we wanted to go to the gym or not. Tuesday would be our main session, where we'd get physical. Wednesday would usually be a rest day. Thursday would be another pretty tough session, but we'd incorporate some team plays. We usually had Friday off, then we were in on Saturday morning for a final run-through before the game on Sunday. The training was spaced out giving us plenty of recovery periods, with a view to us peaking on the Sunday, which was always the most important day of the week.

Shaun was a quiet type of character. You wouldn't hear him shouting and bawling, he would just explain calmly and sensibly what he wanted us to do. Being Australian, rugby league was 'footie' to him; rugby union was 'rugby'. He'd say to me, 'Ah, you used to play rugby, did you? How are you enjoying footie?' I probably got to know him a little bit better later on when I was in the throes of departing. He sat me down and said, 'I don't really want you to go because I think you're a good leader. You're not a dumb footballer by any means.' I got on well with him, and I think he had a nice approach to the game. He treated rugby like a job, very much like I did: he came into work, then went home. You only saw him at the club when he needed to be there, so I could relate to that. I enjoyed playing under him and respected him as a person.

Paul Newlove had joined St Helens towards the end of 1995, and as part of the deal Paul Loughlin, Sonny Nickle and Bernard Dwyer had been transferred to Bradford. Paul Loughlin had been in tears because of the way the club went about it. They'd just called him into the office and said, 'We're going to have to release you, along with Sonny Nickle and Bernard Dwyer.' Paul was a St Helens boy born and bred; he'd been there for about twelve seasons. He was a local celebrity, and even worked at the club as a groundsman, so it came as a massive shock to him.

Paul Newlove was a very quiet character. When he first arrived I shook his hand and said, 'Nice to meet you,' then got on with it. I played on the right-hand side, which inevitably means a lot more defending because most teams are better going from left to right with their plays. Playing on the left, Paul had more of the attacking duties, but I had no problem with that. Paul's a strong player, but a very quiet man. I think he'd be very lost away from his home environment. I remember him telling me once that when he goes on holiday, for two weeks in the Med or whatever, he can't wait to get home. He just doesn't like it at all – doesn't like the food, doesn't like the weather. He's a stereotypical northern lad. When I look at Paul I sometimes think he's not in tune with the modern era. He comes from this little place called Pontefract in Yorkshire, yet he plays for a very high-profile side. He's very introverted, but a tremendous athlete and a terrific player.

Paul was a welcome boost to the ranks, because between the end of the centenary season in January 1996 and the beginning of the Super League in March we had Challenge Cup ties every fortnight. I remember Shaun saying to everyone, 'Let's have a good Challenge Cup,' and a lot of the boys were saying, 'Well, we've got there so many times before and lost, let's really go for it this time.' There was a real determination about the club, so we negotiated a payment structure to take us through to the final and we thought that if we got our act together, started well and avoided Wigan in the first or second round, then we'd have a good chance of going all the way.

We began well with a 58–16 win at Castleford in the first round, and then beat Rochdale Hornets 58–20. At that time the BBC were covering the Challenge Cup and Five Nations on alternate Saturdays, so we had the Five Nations weekends off. Some of the friends I'd made in Rainford at the Red Cat pub – Steve, Tricky and Fish – had never been to a Five Nations game, so one week I said, 'Why don't we go and watch Scotland play France at Murrayfield?' There was no point in going to see Wales, because if we went to Dublin, Twickenham or Cardiff there would be thousands of mad Taffs everywhere. In many ways the best fixture of all is France in Scotland because the French don't take a lot of travelling support, so Edinburgh, although busy, isn't full of pissed-up idiots.

I rang Gavin Hastings to see if he could find us a hotel room for four that weekend. He tried his damnedest and eventually came up with one, so we travelled up and had a glorious weekend. The hotel was fine and we met a lot of nice people. Gavin entertained us at the Watsonians club, and we went back to a function of his in the evening and met up with some old Scottish internationals. My friends from Rainford were not averse to rugby union and recognised the likes of Roger Baird, the ex-Scotland wing.

On the afternoon of the match we walked from the hotel to Murrayfield and sat up in a corner of the stand, and it was then, and only then, that I realised how much I really missed it all. There were cockerels all over the place, as usual, and Scotland came away with a win. I didn't say much during the game, but as we passed the flask of whisky around, one of my friends, Steve, said, 'You miss this, don't you?'

Yes, I did.

CHAPTER SEVEN

Glory Days

During the winter of 1995, the St Helens board had called me in, and asked me, 'How do you feel about going back to rugby union?' I replied, 'Well, if it's right for me, yeah, I'd love to.' They then told me that Bristol had rung them and asked about my availability, and St Helens, like any business, had said, 'If the price is right, we'll sell him.' They went on. 'It's up to you, Scott. We've mentioned a figure to them, and they've said it wouldn't be a problem, so if you can sort something out I feel sure we can do a deal. We'd love you to stay here, though, don't get us wrong. It's just business.' The club hadn't paid anything for me by way of a transfer fee when I switched from rugby union, so they naturally looked on the possibility of selling me on as a good deal.

I went to meet the chairman of Bristol in Gloucester. Mike Burton, who had apparently become involved in the negotiations, was there too. The way this chairman was talking – about anual salaries in the region of £15,000 – I thought he was off his head.

Within five minutes I said, 'Don't insult my intelligence and my integrity. I've been in a professional environment for the last eighteen months, and I get paid for playing rugby, so don't mess me about.' Nothing came of it. I thought to myself, If this is what professionalism is all about in rugby union, then forget it.

Then I met Newcastle's Rob Andrew and Dean Ryan at the Haydock Post House for a chat. They were looking to develop their side and wanted to get into good professional habits early on, so they asked me about the make-up of my week – the rest periods, training etc. We had a general chat and just talked about the logistics of the whole thing and how I thought a professional football club should be run. I had already spoken to Eric Ashton about union clubs being interested in signing me, and he'd said that the St Helens board would be looking for about a £150,000 transfer fee in order to agree to a move. When I mentioned this figure to Rob Andrew, he said, 'Yeah, no problem.' So I told him to ring the club and they started negotiating, but all of a sudden the St Helens board decided they wanted £250,000 instead, which soured the whole process. I decided there and then just to concentrate on rugby league and not get too involved in the wheeling and dealing. If something workable happened on the union front then so be it.

Of course, as soon as I got a little bit of press as a result of the Newcastle approach, things started happening again. Richmond were an up-and-coming club. They had just signed Scott Quinnell from Wigan, and they came up to see me. Simon Elliot, who was then chief executive, and Ben Clarke, their captain, came round to my house and said, 'Right, we're going to sign you,' but then came the same wrangling over the transfer fee as there had been with Newcastle. I think Saints had seen Scott Quinnell leave Wigan for Richmond for a big fee, and they thought – quite understandably

– that if someone out there was prepared to pay that type of money to take him back to rugby union, then maybe they would do the same for me. So I thought it best to forget about the whole thing. I was genuinely happy at Saints, anyway. We were doing well, and I wasn't worrying about my future at that time at all. Having tasted that Five Nations weekend at Murrayfield early in 1996, though, I knew I wanted to go back to rugby union some day, but I was content to see out my contract with Saints. I'd only be twenty-seven when that ended.

I went back to concentrating on the Challenge Cup. Salford had knocked Wigan out, and then we knocked them out in the quarter-final. We then beat Widnes 24–14 in the semi-final, and suddenly we were at Wembley. Usually Saints came up against Wigan in the early rounds of the cup, but this year we'd had a good draw and everything had worked out well. After the win over Widnes, Shaun gave us all a week off, so Sharyn and I jumped on a plane to Savannah, South Carolina, and had a week away. It was great, but by the end of the week I was really looking forward to getting back because St Helens were at Wembley.

But before the Challenge Cup final there was the start of Super League. We were away at Workington in the opening fixture, and hammered them 62–0. Then it was Wigan at home. I'd never been on a winning side against Wigan before, and as always it was a massive game. They got off to a thundering start, and I thought, Here we go again, because last time they'd played us at home they'd beaten us by thirty-two points. They were ahead 16–4 at one point and it looked like it would be the same old story, but we came out for the second half and really blitzed them. It was a good day because we'd perfected a kind of umbrella defence where the outside backs would fly up into the middle of the field and try to cut off Shaun Edwards's long balls and plays. This ploy worked a treat, because invariably we turned him back into the middle of the ruck and he wasn't as effective. In the second half they didn't have any answer to it and we managed to put a lot of pressure on them. They made errors, we capitalised on them, and eventually ran out 41–26 winners.

It was a tremendous result. Saints v. Wigan games are big local derbies, the rugby league equivalent of Liverpool v. Everton. I knew they were important, because every time I'd seen them on Sky there was something special about the atmosphere. When you're part of it, there's an even greater buzz. The players know it's special, and the games bring out the best in everyone. Saints v. Wigan ties take over the whole town; there's more hostility towards Wigan than any other side. When I first experienced it I thought maybe it was because Wigan were so dominant in the eighties, but I soon learned that it's always been like that. I remember reading a book about Tom Van Vollenhoven, the great South African wing who played for St Helens in the fifties and sixties. He wrote about 50,000 people turning up for the Saints v. Wigan derbies. Someone else gave me a book on Saints v. Wigan matches, and it confirmed that in the fifties and sixties the tie would regularly draw huge capacity crowds.

I knew we'd achieved something special when we beat them; even though it was only one game it gave a huge boost to the team's confidence. We showed a lot of grit and character to come from behind, and we proved that they could be intimidated. I reckoned that if we carried on playing like that against the likes of Bradford and Leeds then we'd definitely be in with a shout of the title.

In my matches against Wigan, more often than not I'd be marking Gary Connolly, although sometimes they moved me so that Paul Newlove would mark Connolly and I'd be up against the big fella, Inga Tuigamala. I didn't have a problem with that; I'd just get up into his face and try to be a nuisance. The most important thing when facing Inga was not to let him get up a head of steam. When I first joined St Helens, Apollo Perelini invited me round to Inga's house, and Inga welcomed me to rugby league. I'd been up against him on several occasions during the 1993 Lions tour to New Zealand, and of course to meet him and his family and see how gracious and loving they were was terrific. When I introduced Sharyn to him, he made such a fuss that she felt very much at home. To look at he's a very big, intimidating guy, but he's the gentlest of giants. Mind you, we had a healthy rivalry on the paddock.

But, as I said, in most of the Wigan matches I was up against Connolly, for whom I have the utmost respect. He's a St Helens boy born and bred. He played for Saints before signing for Wigan, which to the St Helens supporters is a cardinal sin, but the way I look at it he did what was best for him and it's been a great move. Whatever club he'd been playing for, he'd still be a Great Britain international, because he's one of the best centres in the world in either code. Everyone raises his game against a class player like Connolly. He's very dangerous, so I always tried never to let him run freely, and when I had the ball I'd always run straight at him. He'd tackle me more often than not, but there were a couple of times when I just ran straight over him. I don't think he's intimidated by anyone, but I gave as good as I got. He was always in St Helens, and I'd see him around and socialised with him on a couple of occasions, but I never felt I got close to him at all. I wanted to get to know him a bit better, but I think he kept me at a distance. A lot of the Saints boys were very close to him, and I was pally with them, but I never got to know the real Gary Connolly, although I enjoyed his company.

Connolly is noted for playing as hard off the field as he does on it. I think his reputation as a drinker preceded him, because when he went to Harlequins, Jason Leonard, noted himself for liking a couple of pints, thought Connolly's drinking wasn't of premiership status. I beg to differ on that one, because I probably had more experience of his drinking than any of the Harlequins boys. They'll probably say that southern lager's stronger than northern lager, but I'm not so sure.

Leisure time is another important facet of the total professionalism of rugby league. In rugby, as in most team sports, in order to bring the best out of everyone you need that time where you relax together and do some team bonding. We slowly got together at St Helens and started to do a bit more of that, and it paid off. I think it was a contributory factor to the club's success in that first Super League season. We started going out together on Tuesday nights, and we simply became better friends. We'd make a point of going to the same place at the same time every week, and we even wore the same clothes. There's not a great deal going on in that area, so I found myself playing dominoes and getting involved in pub quizzes, and stuff like that. We'd also go to places like the Old Road Labour Club to play snooker. It's a fallacy that rugby league players are so professional that they don't drink. I can say from first-hand experience that they drink far more than rugby union players, but by the same token they're more sensible about it. You never see anyone complaining of a hangover.

After seeing off Wigan, we went on to beat Leeds, Bradford and Halifax, which put us in great shape by the time the Challenge Cup final came round, at the end of April. The build-up to that was special. We went to stay in Slough and trained at Eton. Gareth Rees, the Canadian rugby union full-back, was a master there and he brought his class over to watch us training. It was nice to see him again. It was my first experience of Wembley, and I remember thinking it looked a bit small; certainly I thought the changing rooms would be bigger. But it was still the best and biggest day I've had in rugby. People say, 'What about the Lions?' Well, they were good days for sure, but you've got to go a hell of a long way to beat a Challenge Cup final day. It's such a fantastic atmosphere.

When we ran out, everyone was singing and dancing. The St Helens fans were at the tunnel end, and the Bradford lot at the opposite end. There was a drought on at the time, and it had been widely publicised that Yorkshire was having to bring extra water in by tanker, so within five minutes all the St Helens supporters were singing at the Bradford fans, 'Where's your water gone? Where's your water gone?' It was little moments like that that stuck with me.

It turned out to be a real tough battle against Bradford. There wasn't much flair on show, it was all down to which team was going to make the fewest mistakes. I found myself running from dummy half all the time and making those first couple of yards, but we got the bounce of the ball a couple of times. We couldn't lay a finger on Robbie Paul that day. He ran into me twice; each time I was determined to take him down, but each time he just spun away and was gone. He was incredibly elusive.

We went behind, but we didn't panic. The game was so quick that you didn't have time to think about the score really. Bobbie Goulding soon started to pepper the Bradford full-back, Nathan Graham, with high kicks. We got a try from one of them, so we thought, Why don't we do the same thing again? The plan was to get down to their end of the field, play out our sets of six and then put the pressure on them with a kick, either a high one on the full-back or a little grubber. Amazingly, it just kept on working.

We were in the lead with about a minute to go when Bradford

made a break down my side of the field. I was chasing Carlos Hassan and thinking, I'm not going to get there, I'm not going to get there, but I dived and caught him around the bootlaces and managed to bring him down five yards from the line. There were another two tackles to go, but then the whistle went and we'd won, 40–32. Everyone just looked up and shouted, 'I love you!' It was a great day, and when we went on the lap of honour I remember spotting some friends from Pencoed in the crowd. It was fantastic. Saints hadn't won the cup for twenty years. Phil Veivers had been in a final and lost, as had Paul Loughlin – who, of course, was playing for Bradford that day.

I was so elated, but there were a few downers around the corner. Everyone wants to go up the steps first, second or third, but I ended up being one of the last up to receive my medal, so by the time I held the cup up everyone had gone. What was worse, when I got back to the changing room I was selected to go for a drugs test. Drugs tests have been the bane of my career. I seem to get picked out every time. Every time I've played at Wembley I've been selected. So while everyone was celebrating in the changing room I was upstairs, and because I was so dehydrated I had to guzzle about four litres of water straight away in order to produce a sample. I still didn't urinate for about two hours.

By the time I walked out of the tunnel to go to the function it was nearly dark. There was no one else around, so I walked across the ground, thinking, What a day! Only a matter of hours before there had been 80,000 people packed in there; the atmosphere had been electric, but now you could hear a mouse squeak. I walked up the steps, but the function had virtually finished, so I just jumped on the bus, went back to the hotel and sat down all night, because I was just absolutely shattered. Everyone was the same. We had a party back at the hotel where everything was free – well, up to a

Getting the boot – me
aged about twelve months.

Me with Dad and my
sister Claire getting to
grips with a rugby ball.

Me, aged six, with my nan, on holiday in Bournemouth. She had such a big influence on my early upbringing.

The Dolau Primary School rugby team from 1980. I'm on the end of the front row, far right. Adrian Davies, who also went on to play for Wales, is the captain holding the ball.

Me with my mum on holiday at Tenby.

The Pencoed Youth team. I'm second from the left on the back row, and Adrian Davies is next to me on the end.

Mr Serious. On the morning of my first cap for Wales Youth, against Canada Juniors on 8 October 1988.

Wales Youth v. England Youth at Wrexham in April 1990, when I captained the side. From left to right: Jonathan Westwood, me, Richard Brown and Neil Jenkins. We won 12–6, and Neil kicked all our points. Some things never change.

Me and Sharyn. Thankfully, she has no interest in rugby whatsoever.

Taking on the Irish defence during my debut season in the Five Nations, 1991. (*Allsport*)

In action against Southland on the 1993 Lions tour of New Zealand, which was such a good experience after the nightmare of the Wales tour to Australia two years before. (*Allsport*)

After several false starts I eventually sign for St Helens in April 1994. I'm pictured with coach Eric Hughes.

Scoring a try in my first game for Saints, against Widnes at Knowsley Road.

Running hard and straight for Saints in the centenary season. Everything hurt after a game of rugby league, even eyebrows and earlobes. (*Allsport*)

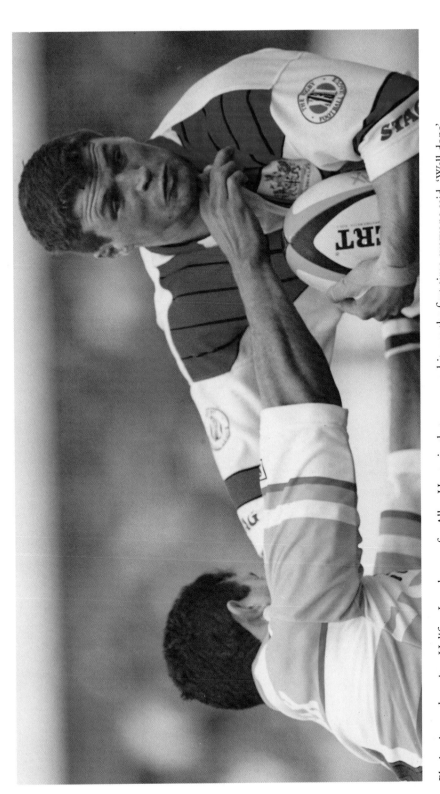

Playing it tough against Halifax. I made a try for Allan Hunte in that game, and it was the first time everyone said, 'Well done'. At the time I didn't know how much winning money meant to a lot of the boys, but winning was everything. (*Allsport*)

The greatest moment in my rugby career: winning the Challenge Cup with St Helens in 1996. Here I am with the boys after beating Bradford Bulls 40–32 at Wembley. Someone has put the lid of the cup on my head. (*Allport*)

Playing for the Lions in the First Test against South Africa in June 1997. Andre Snyman tries to take me on, but I just dump him. (*Allsport*)

Celebrating that historic Lions series victory over South Africa with skipper Martin Johnson, after we'd beaten the Springboks in the Second Test 18–15, thanks to Jerry Guscott's wonderful drop goal. (*Allsport*)

Trying to run
through the entire
England pack during
our 60–26
hammering at
Twickenham in
1998. (*Allsport*)

Taking on my old mate Neil Jenkins when Swansea beat Pontypridd 45–27 on our way to the Welsh Premier League title in 1998. Welsh club rugby just wasn't competitive enough, so we decided to opt out the following season and play the top English clubs instead. (*Allsport*)

Playing for the Welsh team during the sevens competition in the 1998 Commonwealth Games in Kuala Lumpur, with Waisale Serevi looking on. We were beaten by Canada, and it was another bad experience playing for Wales abroad. (*Allsport*)

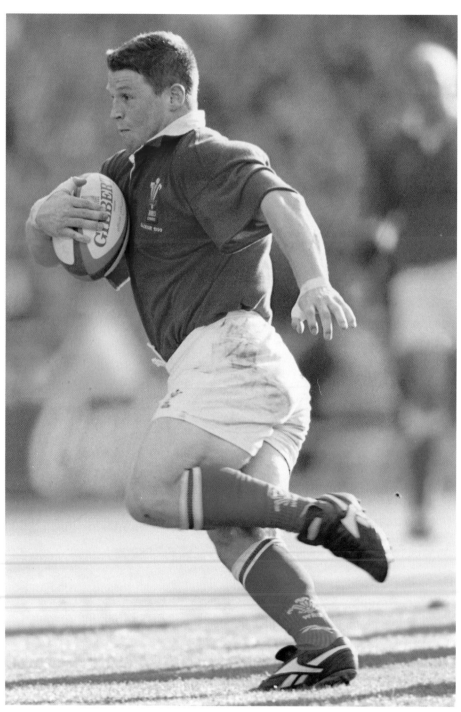

On the charge against England at Wembley in 1999. My last-minute try set up that historic 32–31 victory, but it still took a cool conversion by Neil Jenkins to win it. (*Allsport*)

The Swalec Cup was the only thing Swansea could win after refusing to play in the Welsh Premier League in 1998/99, and we did, beating Llanelli 37–10 in the final at Ninian Park, much to the annoyance of the establishment. (*Allsport*)

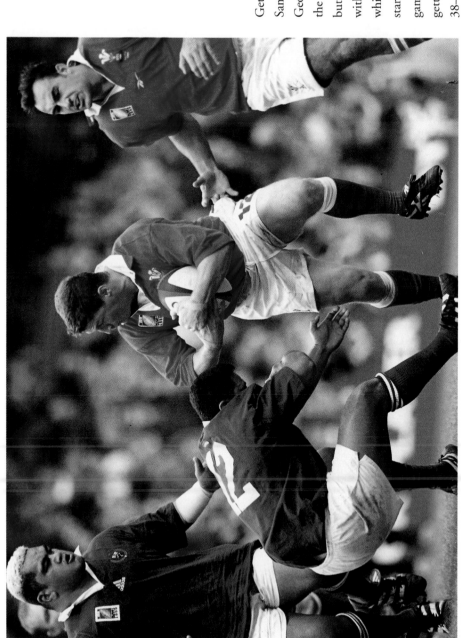

Getting the better of Samoan centre George Leaupepe in the 1999 World Cup, but later he hit me with a high shot which left me seeing stars for much of the game. We ended up getting beaten 38–31. (*Allsport*)

limit, of course; it's not like Saints to push the boat out! There we all were round the table, blazers off, for most of the night, but there wasn't much conversation because everyone was just so drained. I think that the best parties, ironically, are always when you lose, because you can always find solace in a beer after a defeat. I suspect we were all dreading the long bus journey home the next day, too.

So the following day we all piled onto the bus and headed home. As we reached St Helens we had to pull off into Newton-the-Willows on the outskirts, and then make our way through the town. It was pouring with rain, but there was a massive turn-out. Quite frankly, I just wanted to get home and put my feet up. As far as I was concerned the game was finished and my weekend was over, so I didn't really enjoy the parade and having to get up to speak in front of the huge crowd. I was feeling low because of the fatigue and the damp weather, and I think I convinced myself that I was going to catch flu. In fact, that week about half a dozen of us went down with a bug, but some of the other boys, still on a high, were still partying.

I was pleased with myself, though. I reckoned I'd achieved a lot with St Helens in a short time; in the space of two years I'd got my hands on a Challenge Cup winner's medal for which some players had waited ten, even fifteen years. I knew that by doing so I was in an elite band of only a dozen or so Welshmen, and it's something I'll treasure for the rest of my days. I'd also been on the winning side against Wigan for the first time, so things had gone pretty well for me in the last few months.

We had a couple of days off, and then it was time to come back down to earth because we had to get back to the Super League. We had a good side, and I thought we were all playing pretty well. Shaun McRae's training regimes were striking a nice balance, and I knew we would be challenging for the title because we'd started so well, although it was going to take a massive effort to finish first because consistency hadn't been the hallmark of many Saints sides. Usually it was a case of five or six wins and then one or two losses along the way. Looking at the fixture list, it was possible to pick out the tricky ones, like Sheffield away – the type of games you know you should win but could easily lose.

In our first game after Wembley in May we thrashed Oldham 66–18, but then had a really tough game against the London Broncos at Knowsley Road. We were outplayed for about an hour, falling behind 22–8 at one stage, but we soon clawed our way back into the game. I scored one try, and St Helens took the lead with about ten minutes to go. Towards the end of the match I chased Junior Paul down the line. I was in a position to tackle him, but I thought that because he was on the touchline I'd just push him into touch, but I lost my balance, spun and landed on my elbow. I ended up tearing the rotator cuff muscle in my shoulder, which put me out of action for the next six games.

I was booed by a section of the crowd at the start of this game, which I think was due to a recent article in the press about the possibility of my going back to rugby union. I never made any derogatory remarks about the club – I have too much respect for the boys for that – but the rumours had started, and obviously some of the spectators didn't take kindly to the idea that I might be considering leaving St Helens. I think the news left a bit of a bad taste in their mouths, but I was only looking after my own interests. At that time Saints offered me a new, improved deal, which was great. I was due to sign it, but then Swansea came in with an offer, so while I was out with my shoulder injury all the transfer speculation started to bubble up again.

After the Challenge Cup final, when I was walking down the steps to jump on the bus, I had bumped into Terry Cobner, the director of rugby for the Welsh Rugby Union. His father-in-law used to play for Warrington, so Terry would come to the Challenge Cup final every year. I didn't really know him, but he introduced himself to me, and then said, 'If you fancy coming back to Wales we can sort something out. We're going to start putting players on contracts.' I'd already been in touch with Swansea, and they'd told me that the WRU was going to do this and that, but quite frankly I'd heard it all before.

While I was out with the shoulder injury, with permission from the club I went down to Wales and met Mike James, the guy who had called me a 'rugby prostitute' when I left Swansea for St Helens. I was determined to be very open about the whole thing, and I'd said to Saints, 'If you don't get what you want, I'm happy staying. I'll sign that new contract, no problem.' But I'd also told Howard Morris, one of the directors, that if something could be done, I'd rather go back. They'd reiterated their position, which hadn't changed: 'We haven't got a problem with that. It's good business for us, and hopefully it will be good business for you.' So I went to see Mike James, who told me, 'Before we start, Scott, you know all that bullshit when you left? I can tell you now, it's not going to happen this time. This is what we're going to do, and your lawyers can check through it.' They laid out what they were going to offer me, and of course everything then went through my lawyers – St Helens's lawyers. I was getting documents from all sides, but I made a point of reading it all. It was all done very efficiently, and, more importantly, in the right way. A contract with the WRU was part of the deal, but the document contained all kinds of clauses, like privacy clauses, and other things that weren't filled in. I signed mine in front of a lawyer, but it wasn't witnessed by anyone from the WRU and it was never countersigned by them. It wasn't even dated, so effectively it was illegal.

While I was still out with my injury St Helens were beaten by Wigan, which was our first defeat of the season, but they had dropped a point at home to the London Broncos so we were still on top of the league. I returned to the team at the end of June for the match at home to Leeds, which we won 42–16, but then we went to Bradford and got a real hammering, 50–22, and to make matters worse I got sent off again.

We always seemed to get intimidated up there. The first time I played at Odsal Dave Watson and Roy Powell were playing for them and we won. I think it was the first time Saints had won there for a while, and I remember the boys saying what a good win it was. I thought we needed to strengthen our squad because we were struggling to get players on the park, and at Odsal we were without Bobbie Goulding, Chris Joynt and Vila Matautia. Sonny Nickle, one of the players Bradford got from the deal which brought Paul Newlove to Saints, was on the rampage that night and the game was played at a million miles per hour for the first twenty minutes, during which time Bradford raced to a 26–0 lead.

I learned early on in rugby league that people come in for the tackle with flying arms, so you've got to duck. Every time my arm or elbow was raised it was just to protect myself, and of course because I was shorter, I connected more often than not. On this occasion at Bradford I took the ball up and ran into Jeremy Donougher, who collapsed in a heap, which made it look much worse than it was. I had James Lowes in my face screaming obscenities, and the next thing I knew I was in the changing room. I was so disappointed. It was the second time I'd been sent off that year, and I had to go to a disciplinary hearing again, which is always embarrassing. I got a fine and was banned for a couple of matches.

I returned to the team once more on 27 July for the game in

London against the Broncos, which turned out to be my last in rugby league. It was a fantastic match, with the lead continually changing hands right up until the final whistle. I scored a try in the second half; I got the ball about twenty metres out and just forced my way over the line, taking about three defenders with me. When I came back up the pitch after scoring, the boys said, 'Jesus, that was incredible,' but my efforts had resulted in a spiral fracture of the finger, which means I broke it from the base all the way up to the tip. I'd handed someone off, my finger had been twisted like a stick of celery, and it had cracked all the way through. I was in a lot of pain afterwards. It took a fantastic try from Apollo Perelini in the dying minutes to win that match for us, 32–28, and keep us on course for the title.

I didn't, of course, know at the time that it would be my last game for St Helens because I was still in negotiations with the club and Swansea as to when I would be released, but eventually a date was agreed. We had a crucial game against Castleford the following week, and Shaun McRae said, 'Please, Scott, will you play in this one for me?' But my finger was still troubling me, and I replied, 'To be honest, I can't even make a fist with this hand.' The medical staff said they could give me some pain-killing injections to allow me to play, but I told them I'd rather not; a large number of hand injuries take ages to heal, and I didn't want to aggravate mine. I was virtually on the brink of a new season with Swansea, and as it happened I still missed a few of their early games because of that finger injury.

St Helens won their next three games without me, and then it was all down to the final one against Warrington at Knowsley Road. Victory would hand the club the title, and they won easily, 66–14. I wasn't at the ground that day – I can't remember why; there was something on I couldn't get out of – but I watched the game on television. The club was great to me after they were crowned champions. They didn't forget about me, and rang me up later to say, 'We've got your medal here, come and pick it up.' So I went back to the club, and the directors were there all dressed up, and the cameras were there, and I thought it was a really nice touch.

Even though mine was a very short stay in rugby league terms, almost a fleeting visit really, it was a great experience for me and I made a lot of good friends. I had a Challenge Cup winner's medal and a Super League champions medal to show for it, and I even managed to captain the side on a couple of occasions. I was a bit disappointed that I wasn't able to play a fuller role towards the end of the campaign, but it was an absolutely wonderful year for me.

When all the negotiations between me, Swansea and St Helens had been completed, Howard Morris stunned me by letting on a figure the club would have been prepared to pay to keep me. I just couldn't believe it. I told him, 'It's too bloody late now. If you'd said that back in May, we wouldn't have had to go through all this rigmarole, and I'd have stayed.' Saints had, of course, offered me a deal, a good one, but I was going to earn more by going home. If they'd matched that, I would almost certainly have stayed for another eighteen months to two years and fulfilled my contract.

One thing I did regret about my stay in rugby league was that I didn't get the opportunity to play for Great Britain. At the end of the 1996 Super League season there was a tour to New Zealand, and initially I was down as one of the squad members. Everyone was saying, 'You've got a good chance of going on the tour,' and it was something I really wanted to do. Gary Connolly and Paul Newlove were always going to be the first-choice centres because they are two exceptional players, but I was in with a good chance of claiming one of the other places. Of course, I had to think about my future, but it would have been fantastic to have represented Great Britain.

I was in rugby league for two years, and I think I crammed a lot of rugby into that time. I missed some of it with injuries of various descriptions, but although I had a few bumps I certainly wasn't injury-prone. I just got hurt – it's that kind of game. The two medals were proof of my achievements, and I will always be very proud when I look back on my time at St Helens.

CHAPTER EIGHT

Back in Union

G oing back to rugby union just made sense. The clubs were
offering full-time contracts, and with what the Welsh Rugby
Union were offering at the time it all added up to a bit more than
what I was getting at St Helens. And I was glad it was Swansea who
had come up with the deal; I was far happier going back there than
I would have been joining Cardiff or Llanelli, who'd also made
offers.

I enjoyed being back at Swansea, but initially it was very
difficult to adjust. I was looking forward to settling down and
getting back into rugby union, and of course the Lions tour to
South Africa was coming up in the summer of 1997, so that was at
the back of my mind, although I knew I had to get my skates on
and have a good season. As I said, I missed the first two games of
the 1996/97 campaign because of my broken finger, so my first
match back was up in Caerphilly, and I was bored rigid. I said
afterwards that I'd never been so bored on a rugby field. Mike

Ruddock, the Swansea coach, called me into the office on the Monday and said, 'That's not the type of comment I want to read in the paper. Keep it to yourself.' I told him I was just telling the truth. Next up was Pontypridd, and I didn't really enjoy that one either.

There were a lot of new faces at Swansea, but it wasn't long before I settled in. I knew all the coaching staff, though, and was welcomed back by the backroom staff, the old guys who rub you down and look after the kit. They were pleased to see me again, but I can't remember getting a round of applause from the spectators. They're not the most vocal of spectators anyway, but they are very loyal to the club. The Pontypridd match was my first home game, and I think something was announced over the Tannoy about welcoming me back.

The conditioning I was now undergoing for rugby union was a lot different to the conditioning I was used to from rugby league. Because the WRU were now paying part of our salaries, for the first couple of months we had to train four or five times a week with them, then there was the training with Swansea, so it was all a bit over the top. I couldn't settle into it because we were just doing too much. I'd been used to a very regimented training week with carefully mapped-out rest periods, but there were no relaxation or recovery periods factored into our schedule at Swansea.

At Swansea, Mike Ruddock was one of those coaches who, if something wasn't right, would have us out there for two or three hours until we got it right. I've got a lot of time for Mike, but I think at that time he was coming to the end of his tether, and was looking for a new challenge. Only a small number of squad members were full-time professionals, so he was having to juggle the training because some of the guys would train in the afternoon and others in the evening. I think he was looking for a job where he had a full-time squad to work with, full stop. Sure enough, at the end of the season he left to take up the position of director of rugby with Irish provincial club Leinster.

As far as the actual league games were concerned, I didn't find them taxing at all. I'd come off the field, and everyone else would be knackered, but I wouldn't be. I just couldn't get into the game, and it took me a hell of a long time to readjust to the less intense union ways. Playing at inside centre I was looking to provide for the wider guys, which was totally different from rugby league. I wasn't seeing the ball as much as I was used to either, and of course when I did have it I wanted to make an impact, but sometimes that wasn't the right option. I was bigger than when I'd last played union – I weighed about sixteen stones, maybe a little bit more – and I was very comfortable in contact situations; I'd always try to take on a couple of men and then slip the ball out to my centre partner, Mark Taylor. On the whole this worked well, but I didn't really enjoy those first months back. However, I knew that, given a bit of time, I would get used to it.

It wasn't long before I was invited back into the Welsh squad. The team had just come back from another hammering on a tour of Australia, so the emphasis was very much on getting the players fitter. The coaching staff sat down with us, outlined what we were going to do for the next couple of months and showed us the make-up of the week. It was all training, training, training.

Kevin Bowring, the coach, turned to me and said, 'Well, Scott, this is very much like what you were doing at St Helens, I guess.'

'Sort of,' I replied, 'but I can't see any rest or recovery periods in there.'

'Oh, don't worry about that. You'll have plenty of recovery,' he assured me.

But we didn't. The squad trained twice a day every day, and it just got too much. There was a lot of travelling involved as well, some of the boys from Llanelli having to get up really early every morning to travel down to Cardiff. It just wasn't working out, and a lot of players were getting pissed off with it. I certainly was, because at the same time we were doing a lot of work with our clubs as well. The actual quality of the training wasn't that good either. We would do these long interval runs, but there was no emphasis on acceleration or power.

My first game back in the Welsh jersey was against Italy in Rome on 5 October, a game which we won 31–22. The Italians have always been a pretty physical bunch, but I didn't have a particularly good game. I just couldn't get into it; again, everything seemed to be so slow. There were periods in the game when I thought, What am I doing here? Afterwards I felt as if I hadn't really been involved. I was so used to taking the ball from the kick-off in rugby league and making a charge to set it up in midfield. Rugby union had changed a bit since I'd been away, but not that much. Swansea were still doing the same training drills, the same calls were used, and the pace of the game had hardly changed. I think everyone was expecting me to say, 'The game's a lot quicker now,' but it wasn't.

At least Swansea were winning. We recorded a lot of big victories, but then came defeat at the hands of Ebbw Vale and a narrow loss against Llanelli when we'd been on top. We started to come good again as we went into the second half of the season, but by that time I was looking forward to the Five Nations again, because playing international football is really what it's all about.

The press were building me and Allan Bateman up because we'd both just returned from rugby league, but I didn't feel there was any pressure on me at all, and the attention certainly didn't affect my game. It was just ironic that when we won up in Scotland

24–19, the three key players involved in a great try by Scott Quinnell were the three who had come back from league. It was all down to support, angles and hard running, and our defence that day was pretty good as well. It was a massive victory for us away from home, and it was the first time I'd been up to Murrayfield and won. We'd always been on the receiving end of a hammering every other time I'd been up there, so I got a lot of satisfaction from that. We hit a purple patch that day where everything went well for us. We played some good football, and I thought things were really turning around for us.

After the Scotland game everyone was euphoric. It's amazing what an effect a Welsh victory on the rugby field has on the population; everywhere we went people were praising us. But when Wales lose it's terrible; some of the guys even feel too frightened to take their children to school. I've always thought that is a ridiculous attitude to have to sport, because it's all about winning and losing. Sure enough, because we had had one great victory early on, everyone was so excited that they thought we were on our way to great things, and I think we became complacent. Against Ireland, Ieuan Evans scored a try virtually straight from the kick-off and the feeling was, Yeah, we've got these guys! But we were in for a shock. Ireland have a good record against Wales in Cardiff, and they are probably one of the hardest sides to play against because they're always spoiling, creeping offside and defending like maniacs. They kill the ball and turn over a lot of it too, and it's always frustrating playing against them. We could still have won that game at the death, but we'd left ourselves too much to do and eventually lost by the narrowest of margins, 26–25.

Our next game was against France in Paris, one of the toughest fixtures. Colin Charvis was outstanding in that game; he turned over a lot of ball and we found ourselves in with a real chance. On one occasion Jonathan Humphreys only had to catch the ball and we would have scored and won the match, but he didn't and we ended up losing again, 27–22. After that my neck started playing up and I missed the game against England at the Arms Park, which we lost as well, by twenty-one points. That season our record in the Five Nations could so easily have been won three lost one, but it ended up won one lost three. At least we'd been positive throughout the campaign and played a bit of football.

The coaching staff were trying to keep the press off our backs by saying things like, 'We're developing. We're getting better.' I knew Kevin Bowring because he had coached the under-21s when I was playing for them. He is a nice guy, but the step up to the national squad was difficult for him because although he had a lot of new ideas, he'd never managed or coached a first-class side. In my opinion, as I've said, we were training too much before the Five Nations and we trained too much during it too; perhaps if the coaching staff had looked into that side of things a bit more, we would have been in better condition. Dave Clark, the squad's conditioner, is a great guy too, but my physiological make-up is different to every other athlete, yet we all had to do the same kind of workout. He was another guy who didn't have the word 'rest' in his vocabulary; the overriding philosophy was that more training was the way to go. I think if Kevin had coached a first-class side before coming to the national squad he'd have already got to grips with the logistics and problems associated with the day-to-day running of a top-flight side. As it was, we'd have training on a Monday, but everyone would have injury niggles from the weekend and wouldn't be able to put any worthwhile work in, and Kevin always got the hump. He had a torrid time throughout that 1997 Five Nations championship, and when we lost 34–13 to England in the final game in Cardiff he sat us down on the

Monday afterwards and told us he'd had enough. He told us his children were getting picked on at school, which to me seemed incredible. I lived out in the country where no one gave a toss about rugby, so I escaped most of that, but a lot of the boys did have a rough time of it. On reflection, it would probably have been a better idea for Kevin if he'd managed a first-class rugby side and not taken on the burden of running the national team at all.

For most of the year we had certain times when we had to be at Cardiff for training. So we would get there on Monday morning, do a session and then hang around, train in the afternoon, and then go back and train with our clubs in the evening. It was a ridiculous schedule. I found myself spending twelve hours in the car, and for some of the boys who lived out west travelling time increased, so they were just shot to bits.

Having just come from a set-up where everything was carefully thought out and where optimum performance is what you want to attain, and where there's a proper understanding of the necessity of rest and recovery, I really didn't enjoy that period under Kevin Bowring. The Wales squad was just never given the same opportunity, and when you think of the results we had, which were poor, you've got to attribute that to some degree to the training methods that were employed. Even in the week of an international we'd be training Monday, Tuesday, Wednesday, Thursday and Friday. In the end we spoke up and asked if we could at least have Friday off. I said to the management, 'If you're concerned about it, why don't you go and see what some of the best professional clubs in the country are doing?' Just three hours' drive up the motorway you could go and see how Manchester United managed their footballers' time, and what their training schedules were like. Or you could go and see Bradford, Wigan, Saints, whoever. It would have been a simple matter of picking out the bits that were relevant and incorporating them into our schedule. But they all thought they knew best, and did nothing.

Dave Clark's a very knowledgeable guy; he's travelled the world and I'm sure he had some good ideas, so maybe they just didn't have the resources to put it all together, or perhaps they lacked the backing of the Welsh Rugby Union. When you look at Graham Henry now, the WRU have bent over backwards to give him everything he needs, trying to put things in place. I think perhaps Kevin had a master plan the WRU didn't adhere to, and I think that's why in the end they got rid of him.

One good thing about that season was that Swansea got to the Swalec Cup final, where we played Cardiff. On the day of the match it was fine weather where I was, so I took my moulded-sole boots with me. But when I got down to Cardiff Arms Park it was lashing down and the pitch was like a quagmire. Everyone was really astonished that I was wearing moulded soles on such a wet day. The wind was howling through the stadium because they were in the process of dismantling it – the defeat at the hands of England in the Five Nations was the last international match to be played at the Arms Park. Swansea had several opportunities to win the game; we went in at half-time leading 14–9, but in the second half we just lost it and got ourselves on the wrong end of a final scoreline which read 33–26. I can't remember much about that day because there wasn't a full house. It was a shitty day, really, and we lost, so I suppose I erased it from my memory!

We were in with a shout of the title that year as well, but things soon went wrong for us. We'd beaten Pontypridd at home 33–19, but then lost 31–7 at their place – that's when I started having the neck problems which ruled me out of the final Five Nations match. Llanelli then trounced us at home 42–12. I think that was the day one of the Lions selectors came down, but I had to come off at half-time with my neck problem and missed a couple of games. Because of a mixed bag of results in the run-in, we ended up runners-up to Pontypridd in the league.

By that time I'd already had a letter through the post enquiring about my availability for the Lions tour to South Africa. Without hesitation I'd said, 'Yeah, I'd love to go.' They got a preliminary party of about sixty together in Birmingham during the season to explain how the tour was going to work out, and set some objectives. In the meantime they wanted everyone to try to stay fit and play as well as they could. I can't remember the day on which the Lions party was actually announced, or where I was at the time, but, despite my troublesome neck, for some reason I had an inkling that I'd go.

It was particularly pleasing to get selected for that Lions tour because I knew that ex-league people like Alan Tait, Allan Bateman and John Bentley were going. I definitely thought there had been a positive feeling when the party was being selected, and that these guys perhaps had something more to offer than some of the other international players who were vying for a place. I'm sure the selectors realised it was going to be a very hard-nosed, professional tour, and that they needed people in the squad who had experience of that type of approach. I was over the moon at being in the party, more so this time than last time because when I looked at the line-up I knew it was a very strong squad. South Africa were the reigning world champions, and were playing well. I'd been to South Africa after the 1993 Lions tour to play in Naas Botha's testimonial at the Loftus Versfeld stadium, and I had a good week. I thought, This is going to be my type of tour. It's going to be physical, and only the strong are going to survive.

There was a good build-up to the tour. We met up at Weybridge and stayed in a hotel there. It was good to see the guys who had been on the last trip, but there was definitely a different feel to this one. It was far more meticulously planned for a start. I remember Geech saying, 'This is how we're going to win. Everything we do is geared towards winning this Test series.' Because everyone had had a heavy domestic season – in fact a lot of the Leicester boys were still playing the week we arrived at the hotel – we had a team-building week at Weybridge. We were split up into small groups and had to undertake various tasks. It was a bit like *The Krypton Factor*, but it was good, because Geech realised we'd just come off a hard season. 'The last thing I want to do is start flogging you boys,' he said. 'Let's have three or four days of this, and then we'll have a training session before we fly out.' He went on, 'This tour's going to be won, not by what we do on the field, but by what we don't do,' which was very true, because we did a lot of training on that trip but most afternoons were free, so we had plenty of recovery. We weren't flogged by any stretch of the imagination, and we were going into the games very fresh.

I didn't feel like a seasoned professional this time round, but maybe I was compared to some of the guys. There was a bigger Welsh contingent this time, which was good, and I knew most of the squad. I had shared a room with Martin Johnson in 1993 when he came out to New Zealand, and I would spend most of my time in South Africa with Lawrence Dallaglio, Jerry Guscott and Jason Leonard. As I've said before, the English are the best tourists, and it was true of this trip too. They applied themselves more than anyone and were very professional.

That first week in Weybridge was great, and we finished with a sponsored night down the pub where we all got together, chilled out and had a couple of beers. The make-up of the management team was spot-on too: we had Mark Davies, the Welsh physio, on board, and Dr Robson, who had been with us in New Zealand in

1993; on the coaching side, apart from Geech we had Andy Keast, who had coached Natal and knew a lot about South African rugby. Nothing, it seemed, had been overlooked.

Ex-England prop Fran Cotton was also coming with us as tour manager. I knew Fran because a few years earlier I'd done some work for his company, Cotton Traders, when Jerry Guscott, Gareth Chilcott and I were taken to Malibu for a photo shoot. Fran was from Newton-the-Willows near St Helens, and David Young, who used to work for Fran when he was playing for Salford, told me, 'Fran won't take any messing about over there. If things aren't right, he'll sort them out.' He was very well respected in South Africa, and of course he'd had business dealings with the South African Rugby Football Union because they wore Cotton Traders kit for a while. He was definitely the right man for the job, and I enjoyed the way he handled the whole tour.

Of course, being with Geech again was great fun. I knew exactly the way we were going to train and the type of training we would do. We did a hell of a lot of contact work because I think we knew we were going to have to fight fire with fire on the tour, which was fine by me. I couldn't wait to get there.

CHAPTER NINE

Triumph with the Lions

The 1997 Lions squad flew into Johannesburg in May, and from there to Durban, where we spent our first week. We stayed at a really nice place called Umhlanga Rocks just north of the city, and travelled down to King's Park to train. Unlike the 1993 tour, I was picked for the first game, and I was glad because I wanted to make an early impression. I was going to play alongside Jerry Guscott, which was good, but the day before the match I ran into Neil Back in training and I ended up with a massive haematoma on my knee, so I had to take my seat on the bench.

There was a very intense atmosphere surrounding that first game, against Eastern Province at Port Elizabeth. When we got there a British Police XV were playing before us, and a lot of them were from Wales, people like Colin Hillman, so it was great to see them and get a bit of support early on. I enjoyed watching the game, but it was a hostile one. I think everyone was keyed up and the spectators had been drinking. At one point a massive fight broke out on the railway side of the ground, and some of the crowd were climbing onto the caboose of a train and fighting there. The team came through with a brilliant 39–11 win despite all these distractions, and obviously my eyes were on Jerry and Will Greenwood, both of whom had cracking games. Neil Jenkins also kicked off the tour in fine style, as did Rob Howley. I was really disappointed about missing that first game because I had been looking forward to the tour so much, but after some intensive physiotherapy on my knee I knew I'd be playing in the second match against Border at East London.

When we got there the weather had turned nasty and we played in pouring rain. Just after half-time my ankle went, a similar injury to the one I sustained in New Zealand in 1993 in the match against Southland, but this time it felt a lot worse. A guy ran into me, I tackled him and kind of flipped him over, but I must have got my foot caught under me. I thought, Oh no, this is going to ruin things again. By the time I got the sock and my boot off I knew it wasn't broken, but I thought it could be torn ligaments. Dr Robson said the same thing to me he'd said four years before: 'If we don't get this fixed in seven to ten days, you're going to have to go home, Gibbsy.'

I went straight to the hospital and met a lovely doctor who told me that he had seen me play for the Lions in New Zealand and had been so impressed by my performances that he'd named his son after me, which was quite something for a South African to do. That put a smile on my face, as did the diagnosis, which was that I'd strained my ligaments and only needed rest. Dr Robson knew exactly what to do, and I embarked on yet another course of intensive physio.

I missed the next game against Western Province, which was a real cracker. We won 38–21, maintaining our one hundred per cent record, as we'd overcome Border in a scrappy game, 18–14. Jerry and Alan Tait were really flying, and everyone was revved up because we hadn't lost a game and had played some good rugby. I still wasn't fit for the next game four days later at the beginning of June, against Mpumalanga at Whitbank, which we won 64–14, but I was on the bench for the game against Northern Transvaal in Pretoria. We'd had some good victories, but this fifth match of the tour was going to be our toughest game so far. We were at altitude, and with hindsight I think the boys trained too much. Those who didn't play against Mpumalanga, including me of course, came straight back on the bus and trained at Pretoria that night. The forwards were still flying at it the day before the game, and I think it took a lot out of them. You could see there was no spark there.

I thought I'd get on at half-time; I was really, really revved up about getting out on the pitch, because we were playing crap at the time, although we scored some brilliantly worked tries. Bentos (John Bentley) was having a nightmare, and I was sent on to replace him with about twenty minutes to go, but it was too late by then and we ended up losing by five points, 35–30. To make matters worse for me, after the game I got cited for supposedly throwing a punch at their centre Grant Esterhuizen. At that time I still had a bruised forearm so it was strapped up, and the incident looked a lot worse at the instant it happened than on the television replay. I admit I did catch him in the chops, but I was genuinely trying to go for the ball. Geech and Fran said to me, 'We've seen it on the video. It's nothing, don't worry about it.' That's what I thought too, but the more I watched it the more I thought, Hell, it does look bad if you're an impartial viewer; it does look a bit beyond attempting to go for the ball.

I had to go in front of a disciplinary committee. We all got together in a room and everyone was smoking like chimneys, so it wasn't the ideal scenario. Fran and I turned up in our blazers and gave a good account of ourselves, then we went next door to watch the video. They watched it over and over and over again, at full speed and at half-speed. As far as I was concerned it was just a heavy-impact tackle; I went to knock the ball out and caught him on the chin. I knew they were going to find me guilty, though, but I didn't know how long they were going to ban me for. I think they were a little bit miffed at the time because we had just kicked up a fuss about Marius Bosman stamping on Doddie Weir's knee in the Mpumalanga match, which was blatant and ruined Doddie's tour. I think citing me was a bit of a case of them getting their own back. The James Small/John Bentley rivalry was also being stoked up at the time, and there had been a bit of nit-picking and to-ing and fro-ing in the press, so the motivation was certainly there to get one back on the Lions.

I was handed a one-match suspension, so I missed the next game on 11 June against Gauteng Lions, which we won 20–14. As far as I was concerned that match was a turning-point for the tour. I was up in the stand, and there was definitely a lot of hatred directed towards the Lions from the spectators. So it was a tough game in more ways than one, but we came through it, and that's when I knew we would do well in the forthcoming Test series. Bentos was back on form, he was as happy as Larry, and all the guys were there supporting. We went down to the changing rooms after the game and we were all united. Everyone was so chuffed for the boys and their efforts on the field that day.

It was a crucial time for me as well. There were only two more games before the First Test, and I knew that if I was to have any chance of making the Test side I would have to play well in the next fixture against Natal in Durban, the final Saturday game before the Test. I felt I hadn't really made my mark on the tour yet. I'd played forty minutes against Border when it was lashing down and I didn't have many opportunities to impress, then I'd had twenty minutes against Northern Transvaal when we were playing catch-up football. It had been disappointing so far, but Jerry was looking for a rest so I knew the Natal match would make or break my tour. It promised to be the toughest game so far as they had a very, very strong and combative side. They began very well and were, as we thought, very physical, but that suited me. We took them on and ran out 42–12 winners, but the celebrations were marred by an injury to Rob Howley.

When Rob went off I thought he'd just had a bump; we didn't know until after the game that his shoulder had been dislocated. Rob was going to be the Test scrum-half, but he was forced to go home with that injury. I had early set-backs, but at least I was still on the tour and had a fighting chance of playing in the Tests, but when you have an injury like that, you have to go home. It was very disappointing. Rob was a very fit lad. It can't have been easy for him to watch the Test series knowing he could have been part of it. But I thought his replacement, Matt Dawson, was really brilliant on that tour, and he has become a terrific player.

The team to play the Emerging Springboks was picked midweek, and I wasn't in it. Will Greenwood and Allan Bateman were the centres, but I still wasn't convinced that I'd make the Test team because I hadn't exactly excelled against Natal. Having looked at the video *Living with the Lions* since returning to Wales, there's a bit on selection before that first Test where the selectors say, 'We need someone really sturdy in midfield to knock them over.' Up until then we had defended pretty well, but no one had really imposed himself, but at Newlands we needed to be a lot more physical, so I suppose that's why I got the nod.

The Test side was announced the morning after the Emerging

Springboks game, which we won 51–22 to record our seventh victory of the tour. I was in it, which was great, but I thought the team contained a few surprises. I don't know much about forward play really, so Tom Smith and Paul Wallace as props were initially surprise selections to me. However, on reflection it was inspired, because they were absolute rocks on that trip. I felt the same about Jeremy Davidson; I didn't realise the guy could leap like a salmon. I thought Simon Shaw would be in the second row with Martin Johnson, because he had a great game against Natal and he's a big, physical guy. I did wonder whether we might be a little bit lightweight going into that First Test.

I needn't have worried. Our pack was tremendous at Newlands. In the very first scrum Paul Wallace had Os du Randt, the huge South African prop, in all sorts of strife. The game itself went by in a flash. It was a 5.30 kick-off, and when the lights came down it was a weird sensation. The Springboks started well, and it was only the goal kicking of Neil Jenkins which kept us in the game – we actually led 9–8 at the interval. Neil landed another penalty just after half-time, and we were defending well until I missed a tackle on Gary Teichmann. I just went a bit too open on him and he palmed me off and put Russell Bennett over for a try in the corner.

With ten minutes to go we were 16–15 down and it was nip and tuck. Then Matt Dawson went down the blind side, threw Teichmann a dummy and scored. That effectively won the match for us, but just to rub it in Tim Rodber put Alan Tait away and he outpaced the cover to score in the corner. I came off thinking, This is brilliant! One-nil up against the Boks! Despite my missed tackle I was voted man of the match, probably because I managed to get in a few good hits. Andre Snyman, their wing man, took me on once but he was very light and I just caught him and dumped him. The one I was most pleased about was my tackle on the huge

Springbok flanker Andre Venter. He was running down the sideline and I caught him with my left forearm right under the chest; it buckled him and he just crumpled in a heap on the floor and was mooing like a cow. He had to have treatment, which slowed the game down, but there were some big hits all round that day.

I got back to the changing room and sat down. I knew my dad would have been watching the match at Pencoed rugby club, so I rang through, but when I said who I was, the poor woman at the other end said, 'Oh, come on, he's over in South Africa. I've just seen him on television!' This was just minutes after the final whistle, and you could tell there was mass euphoria at the club. I spoke to my dad briefly; he said, 'Well done,' and then had a few words with one of my mates. They were all just steaming. It was an awesome day. It was the same kind of euphoria I'd experienced after winning the Challenge Cup final, but this time I was able to enjoy the celebrations because I didn't get tested for drugs.

There was a huge sense of achievement, but we knew on the Sunday that there would be a big inquest by the local media on the Springboks performance. Not surprisingly, they were saying it was more a case of the Boks losing the match rather than us winning it. Geech had known exactly what the Springboks were about. He'd said to us, 'These guys are very, very proud. They'll just want to run at you, they won't use their heads, they'll just want to be physical and out-muscle you. That's all they'll try to do.' And he was absolutely right. Because we were physically smaller compared to them, they just thought they could out-muscle us, which is what they tried to do in that First Test. They all wanted to be heroes that day, and it just didn't work for them. We knew that if we got stuck into them we wouldn't have a problem. It was evident that all these big guys they had were as human as everyone else if you ran at them and tackled them. They were a very big side, even the centres like Japie Mulder, but the harder and faster they came, the happier I was.

The next game, the following Wednesday, was against Orange Free State in Bloemfontein. We won easily 52–30, but the victory was again marred by serious injury, this time to Will Greenwood. He got caught and was hurled to the ground and hit his head on what was a very hard surface. We didn't realise how bad it was until we got to the dressing room. Will had been knocked unconscious and could have died but for the excellent work by the medical team. It was the end of his tour.

For the Second Test at King's Park, Durban, the South Africans made a few changes. Both their centres had been injured so they brought in Percy Montgomery and Danie van Schalkwyk. Our team was the same. Geech was brilliant in the build-up to that match: 'This is the opportunity to do it now. Why take it to the Third Test in Johannesburg, the home of South African rugby, where we'll probably lose? Let's do it here, now.' It made perfect sense. Before we left the hotel for every game, Fran would say a couple of words and Geech would always sit down and get everyone very emotional about the game. We'd had terrific support throughout the tour, and Fran would often read out all the faxes that had been sent from back home. One was from an old lady in England whose husband had played for the 1938 Lions. Motivationally, it was brilliant. We'd also had one from the Prime Minister, and one from Rugby League headquarters wishing us all the best, so we knew everyone back home was supporting us. It was a time of the year where there was no soccer on at all, and I think everyone was supporting the Lions. It was absolutely mind-boggling, and we relished it.

We knew the Springboks were going to try to speed up the game and out-muscle us in that Second Test. They started very strongly, and I thought, Here we go. Van Schalkwyk and Montgomery were in our faces all day, and I remember sticking my elbow out once and catching one of them right in the throat, because he had just run straight at me. I said to myself, 'Don't be an arsehole! If you want to win this game, you've got to play football!' Jenks landed a couple of penalties, and Joost van der Westhuizen scored a try for them, so we were leading 6–5 at half-time. Just after the break Taity went up for a kick and ended up flipping the ball to Percy Montgomery, who strolled over for an easy try. Luckily, their goal kicking was as bad as it had been in the First Test, but Jenks was outstanding and made them pay for any indiscipline. We didn't have many opportunities to run with the ball, but I think we got to a stage where we knew we could win the Test series if we just defended with all our might. A huge emphasis had been placed on quality, sustained defence throughout that trip, and nowhere was it more important than in that Second Test. We were all over the place, tackling like demons.

I suppose the highlight for me was my collision with Os du Randt. I'd got the ball from a drop-off by Gregor Townsend and was trying to edge outwards to link up with Jerry, but du Randt was smack bang in front of me. People have since said that I could have side-stepped him, but I couldn't. If I'd been a few more yards away I could have edged out and offloaded the ball before the tackle, but he was right in front of me. I hit him full on and must have caught him in a soft spot because he just collapsed on the deck and started moaning. I didn't feel a thing, but it obviously hurt him. A lot of the boys were walking past him, saying, 'Get up, you fat bastard.' It obviously made an impact on the people who saw it too, because so many now come up to me and want to talk about it. Perhaps that moment lifted the guys, but you don't really know at the time. Certainly no one came up and gave me a pat on the back. It was just another small victory over the South Africans, another one biting the dust.

They drew level when John Bentley missed a tackle on Andre Joubert, who scored in the corner. It was 15–15 with about seven minutes to go. Gregor Townsend almost scored under the sticks, but they managed to close him down. Then we won a line-out, and Matt Dawson threw the ball back to Jerry. I think he could have closed his eyes and dropped that goal, it was so smooth. I didn't care how much we were under the cosh, after that drop-goal I knew we'd won because I was still feeling fresh and I could tackle anything. When Jerry landed his kick I sprinted like hell over to him and jumped on him; only Jerry could have dropped a goal in a situation like that.

After that, of course, we were really under pressure, and everyone kept asking the referee how much time was left. Eventually he told us to kick the ball out and time would be up. We had a twenty-two drop-out at the time, so Jenks kicked it out on the full, but the referee brought everyone back for the scrum. I could see the forwards thinking, 'What the hell has Jenks done that for?' They didn't know what the referee had said, but as they went down for the scrum, he blew up. The sense of elation and achievement was incredible. Everyone was jumping around. All the guys came running off the bench; it was brilliant. We had a lot of support by then, so we did a lap of honour. There must have been a crowd of about 60,000 in Natal that day, and as we came up behind the posts something drew my attention to a small section of the crowd, and there was my friend from Rainford in St Helens, Steve Hawley. It was so chaotic I could hardly hear a thing, but I did pick out a little whistle. Every time he phones me he pretends he's ringing from Australia and tries to copy that whistling sound you sometimes hear on long-distance calls. I could hear this bloody whistle above everything.

After the match I think everyone stayed at King's Park because there were barbecues and other things going on, but myself, Lawrence Dallaglio, Jerry Guscott and Jason Leonard headed off. We met up with the Sky television crew and found this little quiet wine bar, a jazz place called Beanbag Bohemia. We had a nice quiet drink there and then ended up watching the Mike Tyson fight on television, before heading back to Umhlanga. I was still on the beach at twelve o'clock the following day, enjoying Lion beer with our physio and a couple of the other lads, with the team bus due to leave at 12.30. But none of us slept that night – that's how massive the day was.

What followed was a week of hell. We went up to the Vaal river, and everyone went down with something. A couple of us contracted flu, because all the rooms were damp and the heating was only working on certain floors. Coincidentally, the only areas not working properly were the floors the Lions were on, so there were all kinds of conspiracy theories flying around. A lot of the boys in the squad who hadn't played in either Test – like Neil Back and Tony Underwood – got their wish, because of stomach bugs, flu and a few injuries sustained on the field.

On the first day of July we beat Northern Free State 67–39, and then turned our attention to the final match of the tour, the Third Test in Johannesburg. It was fast. We just couldn't cope with the pace of the game, having been celebrating and convalescing all week. Jerry broke his arm that day. We kept plugging away all through the game, but eventually went down 35–16. I think that deep down we knew it didn't matter because we'd already won the series. I know the South Africans were going on about the fact that they had scored ten tries to our four in the series, but that doesn't mean a thing really. By that stage everyone just wanted to get home; it had been a long trip and we'd been up against it the whole time.

At the end of a big, very tough year, to achieve something like a series win on South African soil was marvellous. As Geech always says, 'Thirty years down the road, you'll bump into one of the squad members, and there'll be that glance, the knowledge that you were involved in something special.' It was the best rugby trip I've ever been on. The sense of camaraderie, the togetherness, the fulfilment and the achievement were out of this world.

The only sad thing for me was that my dad wasn't there to see it. He wanted to come out, but in Durban there was a definite threat of crime, and knowing my dad as I do, I knew he wouldn't enjoy it. He enjoyed the 1993 trip so much, but South Africa is nothing like New Zealand; it's nowhere near as friendly. So he didn't come over, but I think maybe he regrets it now.

But as I said, it was a brilliant trip. There was a lot more responsibility on the players this time round, and a much more open style of management. We set out the rules and all the parameters of how we wanted to be treated and how we wanted things to progress. I remember when we were training in Durban we had a very tough week, and some of the boys were saying, 'I could do with a beer, I could do with a night out.' I was in one of the groups responsible for the well-being of the players, along with Lawrence and Johnno, and we said to Fran, 'I think the boys could do with a night out.' Fran said, 'I haven't got a problem with that. You all go out and have a good night, but make sure training tomorrow is up to the standard we've set.' That was the kind of responsibility and trust we had between us. Above and beyond that, we made a rule that we'd eat out of the hotel once a week as a group. We went to some lovely restaurants, and it brought everyone closer. At the hotel, of course, we had a separate menu from the rest of the guests because all our food was geared towards performance.

And beyond that, we did whatever we wanted to do at night-time. Jerry, Jason, Lawrence and I would sometimes eat in the hotel and sometimes go out and have a couple of bottles of wine, but everything was in moderation, certainly until after the Second Test, when everyone naturally over-indulged a bit. Afternoons were left open; those who preferred to stay active and wanted to go to the gym and work out could. Most of the time I, Taity and some of the other guys would go and do a circuit; others went fishing; some went and played golf. The only thing some of the other guys did that I regret not doing myself was flying down to Dye Island, a waterway of shallow waters where there's a big seal colony – and, of course, where there's a seal colony there's a lot of great white sharks. Some of the guys went down there in a cage, which I really wanted to do, but it was on the eve of the First Test so I couldn't go. I'm glad I couldn't, actually, because the guys who did go came back absolutely shattered.

On the whole I think some of the South Africans we met were very arrogant about their country. They would say to us, 'Isn't this the best country in the world?' To them it probably is, but most of it wasn't my cup of tea. The Durban coastline was nice, but I had had visions of something like the Californian coastline; to me it was more like the Blackpool coastline, with a lot of sixties and seventies architecture. I was disappointed, because I'd painted a picture in my mind of something grander. But when you looked at the stadia, there was no expense spared. Cape Town was very nice, and parts of the bay were wonderful. Areas like Stellenbosch and the Paarl are lovely. But on the whole I wasn't particularly attracted to it, and the South Africans couldn't get to grips with that. I was only being honest, saying, 'No, I don't think it's as nice as parts of Australia and New Zealand, America, or parts of Europe,' which was perhaps a little undiplomatic and didn't go down too well. But they were so bullish about their country; in fact, they were bullish about everything. Throughout the tour, apart from a few genuinely nice people we met, we didn't get any praise from the South Africans. They were blaming the results on coaching problems, their players, just about everything really; there were no pats on the back for the way we performed. But we didn't care.

We got on well as a squad, but obviously some got on with certain people better than others. In Alan Tait's book, he writes that he and Jerry didn't get on. Maybe that was a clash of personalities. Alan is from a background which is very, very professional, and if he's got a little niggle he'll go out and do as much training as he feels he needs to to iron the problem out. If at the end of the day he pulls the performances out, I don't have a problem with that at all. Jerry probably felt he was shirking his team responsibilities, but the reality was far from that. I spent a lot of time with Taity in the gym, and if he'd done enough in the morning for his legs that was fine, but in the afternoon we'd work hard and do an upper-body circuit, a lot of boxing stuff, so maybe Jerry just didn't see that part of it. Taity put in just as much work as everyone else, and it was a time when I got closer to him.

I got on well with Jerry. We'd become friends on the 1993 tour. I don't profess to be his best buddy or anything, but I enjoy his company. Jerry's a good guy, a focused, dedicated professional on tour. When it comes to the games, he switches on, does his bit and, like me, switches off afterwards, which is where I can relate to him because he's probably one of the very few who can do that, apart from myself. They all say that he's a difficult character to get on with, but I've never found that.

John Bentley was by a long stretch the leading personality on tour, as everyone who's seen the video *Living with the Lions* knows. I'd played against him in my rugby league days, and had heard him 'terrorising' people. That was his trademark. When I was playing for Saints I could hear him saying to Allan Hunte or Danny Arnold alongside me, 'I'm gonna terrorise ya!' in that broad Yorkshire accent of his. When I heard it out on the field in South Africa, I just buckled up laughing, because I wondered just what on earth the South Africans would make of it. They probably couldn't understand a word he was saying. Bentos was a scream on tour. He put in some marvellous performances, but when his performances, in his eyes, weren't up to scratch, he went off tour. You just wouldn't hear from him. Everyone knew when Bentos was back on tour though – he could whisper over three fields. But you need a blend of personalities on tour, and we had that and it certainly contributed to our success. Martin Johnson, for instance, is a very quiet character, very shy, an insular type of guy who just gets on with it and leads by example. Bentos was more outgoing; he had to say his piece and get revved up. We had a good mix in the squad.

On our way from the hotel in Sandton to Johannesburg for the Third Test, with the series won, the team bus was dead quiet except for a tape playing, I think, R. Kelly's 'I could dream, I could fly'. I was sat next to Bentos and he was bawling his eyes out. 'It's just been such a long time. I miss the kids,' he was saying. Even though there was only one game left, just eighty minutes, and then we were going home, he still got emotional about missing his kids. The man wore his heart on his sleeve. I thought he'd come back to South Africa and be a chat-show host or something, because he was bosom buddies with all the press, the South Africans, anyone who was anyone. They all knew Bentos; he was a lovely character, a great team-mate, and I liked his passion and humour. Of course, there was this thing with him and James Small – I suppose two not dissimilar characters. James Small was a bit of a pin-up boy in his homeland, and he and Bentos had a few confrontations. Perhaps it would have been better if they'd settled their differences on the field of play, rather than spouting off in the media.

A lot has been made of the contribution of the ex-rugby league players, like Bentos, to the success of the Lions, but I don't think it was that significant really, because everyone was so focused. When you look at it, I missed a tackle on Teichmann in the First Test which led to a try, Taity made a mistake in the Second Test which cost us five points, and Bentos made a poor attempt at a tackle on Andre Joubert in the same game to concede another five, so we all made massive blunders. Nonetheless, I think we all contributed to the cause, but the press probably made more of it than the squad did. We were just integral parts of a quality squad, and all contributed fairly to it. There wasn't one waster on that tour, whereas in 1993 there were a few hangers-on.

On the last day of the tour the sponsors, Scottish Provident, put on a free bash for everyone. We all met at lunch-time, reflected on the tour and just chilled out. We drank and drank and drank until it was time to go to bed – the proverbial end-of-tour piss-up really. Contrary to details in a subsequent *News of the World* story about the tour, I wasn't aware of anything going on as far as taking drugs was concerned, and I didn't hear any talk of it at any time on the trip. If we're accused of drinking too much alcohol on that last day, I'd put my hands up and plead guilty, but drugs? No.

I found out that day that I'd been voted Man of the Series by all the sports writers. Jenks won the series for us really with his kicking, but I suppose they thought my contribution was valuable. I was pleased with that. It was a nice accolade, especially as I'd started off so poorly.

CHAPTER TEN

Low Days Again

After getting home from the Lions tour my next big fixture was my marriage to Sharyn. She's from Bridgend, and I'd known her for several years. When I'd signed for St Helens in the summer of 1994, after about six months she'd come up and started to work in Manchester, before getting a job in Wigan.

She doesn't like rugby, which I think is brilliant. She doesn't know one end of a rugby ball from another. Unlike most wives she just doesn't want to get involved. She's probably only been to half a dozen games since being with me, and every time she's been she hasn't watched the game – she's been too busy looking at what everyone else is wearing. I think it's great, because when I come home I can immediately relax. I honestly don't know if I could handle a girl who was into rugby.

When I got back from South Africa early in July, we had just ten days to get everything organised. The wedding was due to take place in Bridgend, followed by a reception in Cardiff. Only sixty guests were invited, so it was a special day – basically just friends and family. But still, I'm not one for a great deal of fuss, and to be honest I'd have preferred just to go away and get married on an island somewhere, but Sharyn wanted a traditional wedding. It didn't really bother me. I would have gone in my T-shirt and jeans if I'd been allowed, instead of the tuxedo I ended up wearing.

Before I knew it we were back into another season of rugby with Swansea. I was still feeling pretty shattered from the Lions tour, and I hadn't had a break from rugby for a couple of years. Swansea had signed a New Zealander, John Plumtree, as their new coach. He had actually played for Natal, and I'd met him briefly when I was in South Africa with the Lions. I didn't know how to take him at first when I went down to Swansea, because his opening line was, 'You've finished the Lions series, now it's back to work. I'm the chief here.' I thought to myself, Oh great – just what I need! But I think he's been a revelation for Swansea. He's played at the top level for Natal in the Super 12 series and he brought all his experience and the training methods he learned from Ian McIntosh, the former Natal and South African national coach, to the club. Under Mike Ruddock, and with the Welsh team, we would be training all the time, but when John Plumtree arrived all that stopped. He cut the length of our sessions to an hour and a quarter, and then he reduced the number of sessions we had each week.

We then got Phil Richards on board, a conditioning coach from west Wales, and he was very, very knowledgeable and on the same wavelength as the players. We began to concentrate a lot more on explosive running and tackling; he also spent time on our footballing skills. His remit was to get us more athletic and more powerful, and certainly as a result of Phil's efforts the team was going into matches that season feeling fresh and looking forward to the game, and we were by far the best conditioned side in the league.

I missed the opening game of the season at Ebbw Vale, which we won 47–11, but then we lost 25–22 at Llanelli in October, beat Cardiff 31–22 in December, and just after Christmas we drew at home with Pontypridd, 24–24. It was a bit of a mixed bag, but overall very successful, and we finished the season very strongly, beating Bridgend 71–19 early in May and winning 45–27 at Pontypridd in our last league match. That meant we won the championship by six points from Cardiff, and our success was largely due to the fact that we were in better shape, and we'd rested sensibly through the season.

We didn't do so well in the European Cup though, finishing third in our pool of four and failing to qualify for the knockout stage. We lost twice to Wasps and away at Glasgow and Ulster, and the board weren't too happy with our performances. We were on course to win the Swalec Cup though, but a 27–13 defeat at the hands of Ebbw Vale in the quarter-finals in what was a very physical contest put paid to any hopes of Swansea doing the double. But we finished worthy champions that year, which confirmed we were consistently the best side in Wales. The club played some good football that season, and the players are a good, sensible bunch of boys. We work hard at our game, but not every day; just because we're full-time professionals it doesn't mean to say you have to be at the club eight hours a day. The most important training session of the week was the game, and that's what we always focused our attention on.

My first international of the 1997/98 season was against Tonga on 16 November at Swansea, which Wales won easily 46–12, but the next international was a far more formidable challenge. Because the Millennium Stadium was being built we were playing our home games at Wembley, the first of which was against the touring New Zealanders on Sunday, 29 November. We stayed at a hotel in Burnham Beeches, near Slough, which is where the England football team stay, but I think we'd have been happier staying in London somewhere because there's a lot more to do there. Kevin Bowring came up with the idea that on the Friday night we'd have Welsh personalities coming in, having dinner with us and speaking about their experiences of trying to battle against the odds. We had people like Simon Weston, the Falklands War veteran. It was all very interesting, but nothing at all to do with rugby; the evening was more like an audience with Simon Weston, with us posing questions on how he coped in terrible circumstances.

Kevin had also invited the chief executive of Tower Colliery, who told us about how his company successfully took over the running of the pit. It was nice to sit down with people like that, but it really didn't have anything to do with how we would play the game against the All Blacks. We may have developed a bit more of a sense of togetherness as a result, but it didn't serve any real purpose, and I'm sure the boys would rather have had Tom Jones come to the hotel to talk to us about his experiences with Elvis and working in Hollywood and Las Vegas. I've nothing against our guests that evening, but the chief executive just went through all the details of how the acquisition was funded, and it wasn't the type of stuff we wanted to hear really, not the kind of thing that would really stimulate us ahead of an important game. So Kevin's idea died a death.

As it turned out I only lasted twenty-six minutes against New Zealand because I got a cut above my eye and had to go off. They hammered us 42–7 as well, so it wasn't a very happy return to Wembley for me.

We didn't have a game on the opening weekend of the 1998

Five Nations championship that season, so we played Italy at Llanelli and won narrowly, 23–20. At that time S4C were televising the Welsh domestic league and at their behest the games were kicking off at 5.30. As they were also covering the Wales v. Italy match, that was also scheduled to kick off at 5.30. These late kick-off times weren't exactly popular with the players, and I couldn't fathom why 5.30 on a Saturday evening should be considered a good time to start showing live football. If you're trying to target a family audience, why choose a time when grown-ups are usually getting ready to go out, or feeding their kids and putting them to bed? At that sort of time you're also competing against prime-time programmes like *Baywatch* and *Gladiators*, so I couldn't see the point of it. We certainly didn't enjoy playing at that time on a Saturday evening, and as it turned out it was one of those games where we just couldn't put anything together. We ended up scraping the win thanks to a great try from Gareth Thomas, but Kevin Bowring blamed the poor performance on me and Scott Quinnell. He said we hogged the ball too much, but we had to because no one else was doing anything with it.

I wasn't really enjoying international football at that time because of the structure of it all. Training just seemed a burden all the time. What made it worse was that I could compare it with my experiences with the Lions in South Africa, which had been so good. There was so much personal responsibility put on us by the Lions management and we were treated like grown-ups, whereas in the Welsh camp at that time we were all treated like kids. Of course, when you treat people like kids they tend to act like kids. I just didn't feel any sense of enjoyment in that squad. The management were always trying to pick holes and find excuses, and it was breeding discontent and negative vibes. Playing for your country is supposed to be the highlight of everyone's career, but playing for Wales at that time was anything but.

All of which didn't augur well for the Five Nations, yet in our first game against England at Twickenham we started like a house on fire. We scored two tries and were 12–6 up after half an hour, but then things went horribly wrong. England scored three tries in seven minutes towards the end of the half, and we ended up losing the match 60–26. I actually scored a try in the second half, but that was little consolation as England rattled up a record score against us.

The vibe all week had been, 'We're all in this together'. But of course when we got hammered, all the coaching staff were saying, 'You disappointed us today. It's your fault.' It was a ridiculous attitude to take. We didn't purposely go out and concede sixty points. We felt like retorting, 'Maybe your coaching isn't up to scratch.' It wasn't a happy camp to be in. When we got back to training the following week Kevin Bowring said the pressure of it all was still affecting his family and his children, who were now afraid to go to school. He then asked one of the players how he felt about it all, and got the reply, 'I've had a gutful. Here's my jersey – if anyone else wants it, they can have it.'

I played in the next game against Scotland at Wembley, which we won 19–13, but I had to pull out of the rest of the matches because of my niggling neck problem. Apparently a journalist had asked one of the senior Welsh Rugby Union officials, who he didn't name, about my fitness, and the reply was, 'I think it's a joke. I think he's putting it all on.' The journalist told me, and I said, 'I'm glad he didn't say that to my face, because I would have put him straight.' But that was the kind of thing which was going on at the time, and it was very bad for morale.

I think maybe deep down the Welsh Rugby Union knew how much unhappiness there was around, and that they needed to create a different environment with a more positive vibe. Along with some of the other guys, I was thinking that if it carried on like this, I'd pack it in. I play rugby to enjoy it, and if I'm not enjoying it I might as well give someone else a go. The feeling contrasted so sharply with my experience at club level at the time. I was enjoying my rugby so much at Swansea and felt I was contributing to our success. There was no feeling of success about the Welsh team.

Despite the good times at Swansea, though, there were times when I wished I'd stayed with St Helens a bit longer. I enjoy rugby league and watch it regularly, and I'd love to go back. I know it wouldn't be the same now; for a start I'd be under more scrutiny and more pressure, and of course I'd be a little bit older. Rugby league is fast becoming a young man's game. But I remember how, soon after I returned to rugby union, I was invited to the wedding of Anthony Sullivan, the St Helens winger, and I met up with all the Saints players again and not one of them shunned me. It was great, and every time I watch the Saints play I get a special feeling. There's a Welsh word, 'heraith', which means 'longing'; I have a longing to be part of St Helens again. When I see a guy like Sean Long, the St Helens scrum-half, I think to myself, I bet he's a lovely player to play with.

Lots of union players say to me, 'Oh, I'd love to have a crack at rugby league,' but I tell most of them to forget it because they wouldn't be able to handle it. They've had it too easy in rugby union, especially in Wales and England. Most of the guys at Saints are full-time professionals, but they are earning peanuts compared to half the squad at Swansea – and Swansea are tightly budgeted pay-wise, nothing like Cardiff or the bigger English clubs. These rugby union boys don't know how good they've got it; they don't know what real work is, and I reckon they couldn't hack it. Of course there are exceptions – look at Jonathan Davies. Everyone in rugby league said he would never make the grade because he was too small, but he did. Jonathan had great natural talent, speed, pace and all the skills, but he was a tough bastard as well. Rugby league guys are hard players, full of integrity, and they do feel a bit of resentment towards their rugby union counterparts because of the high profile that union gets, which is understandable. The English union players get a lot of press, and I think the rugby league guys have a right to feel hard done by because half of them are prima donnas. I would stand up for any Super League player before I'd stand up for any rugby union player.

I still play as hard now as I did up north, but in union you just don't get physically bashed about as much. Even with the Lions at Test level you don't get hurt as much as you do playing rugby league. Playing the likes of Wigan, Bradford or Leeds is tough, but even when you're up against one of the lesser sides like Workington you're still going to get tackled, and you've still got to make tackles. It all takes its toll. Everything hurts after a game of rugby league: your ears, your eyebrows, your whole body. I could hardly walk up the stairs for days following a match, but I loved it. It was far faster than union and more my type of game. In rugby union I've learned to be a better footballer, more of a provider, and that's essential in terms of prolonging your career because if you're constantly running into people you're not going to last two minutes. But I loved the physical aspect of rugby league; I couldn't get enough of it. I remember one of the St Helens directors, Tom Ellard, saying to me once, 'When are you going to learn to side-step?' I replied, 'Well, Tom, believe it or not I used to side-step, years ago.' Trouble was, I just got more satisfaction out of running at people – and, of course, I enjoyed the tackling. I would get hit in every game but I wouldn't shy away from anything. In nearly every other tackle you would get winded, but that's what's special about the game: it takes your body to the limit.

When I look back, I reckon I took the easy option by coming back home, but I was only doing that to secure a better future for myself and my family when my playing career ended. That's the one thing rugby league can't offer its players: an opportunity to get employment beyond rugby. That's largely due to the state of the economy in the north. In rugby union you're moving in far bigger circles and your chances of getting a job outside rugby are quite good. That's why I think somebody like Anthony Sullivan, who had a very good spell in rugby union with Cardiff in the 1998/99 season, would eventually like to come to rugby union full-time. He's got the charisma and the intelligence to make something of himself beyond rugby, whereas up in St Helens or Warrington I don't think he'd be able to find a suitable occupation after he finishes playing. Rugby league gives you so much satisfaction while you're playing, but afterwards you're left out in the woods on your own. Rugby union will open more doors for you, and that's a fact.

I still think of that Challenge Cup final with Saints, and one day I'd like to go back and at least savour it all again as a spectator. I remember after the Wales v. Samoa game during the rugby league World Cup I met Freddie Tuilagi, who now plays for St Helens. He'd come down to Cardiff to support his fellow Samoans, and I caught sight of his Super League ring, which he'd got for winning the Grand Final against Bradford a few weeks before. I thought to myself, I'd like to have one of those.

But for the time being I had to focus my mind on union, despite the domestic season having finished. A tour to South Africa had been scheduled, and all the players were sent forms by the Welsh Rugby Union enquiring about availability. Immediately I thought I couldn't refuse to go, because I was convinced that by doing so I'd be breaking my contract with the WRU. I told Swansea that I wasn't fit enough to go to South Africa and asked the board for advice. They confirmed what I'd thought when they said, 'Well, you probably have to say yes because you're obliged to by contract.' So I filled in my form saying I was available. Of course, when the squad was announced there was no way I could go because of my neck problems. You would have thought someone from the medical staff would have had the sense to tell the selectors I was still injured before they made their final choices, but in the end it was me who had to go to the WRU and explain to them about my ongoing treatment for trapped nerves, and why I'd said initially that I was available to tour. After they'd heard me out, the WRU simply said, 'Why didn't you just tell us in the first instance that you weren't thinking of going because of your neck?' So I pulled out of the squad. It was a good move for me, because apart from my sore neck I'd had a tough year, and the last thing I needed was to tour South Africa again so soon after the Lions' exploits.

I'm not averse to touring – I love touring; it can be brilliant fun – but I don't want to do it every year. I do wonder why unions insist on organising a tour every year, because it just doesn't make any sense. I've only been on tour once with Wales, in 1991, and that wasn't a great experience. I do enjoy playing rugby, and I want to carry on with my career as long as I can. I'm not going to sacrifice it or risk curtailing it because of the pressures of these tours which keep cropping up every summer. I just don't see any point. If there was a structure or routine to it, like Lions tours – if it was every other year, say, or even once every three or four years – then there would be something special about the trip, and everyone would get behind the squad.

So, as I said, I took a welcome break that summer and didn't watch any rugby at all. I didn't have the faintest idea about what was going on in South Africa – although, perhaps unsurprisingly, Wales had a bad time out there.

CHAPTER ELEVEN

The Rebel
Season

The 1998/99 season proved to be a momentous one for me, both at club and international level. As I said, I didn't tour South Africa with Wales during the summer of 1998 because I'd been playing hard, non-stop rugby since returning to union, and I felt I needed a break to let my body recover.

I returned to training with Swansea early in July. It was then that our coach, John Plumtree, told me that the club might have an option of playing in the Allied Dunbar Premiership rather than the Welsh Premier League. It came as a great surprise to me, but a pleasant one. He said, 'It's not finalised yet, but we don't want to be playing in this Welsh Premiership any more, do we?' No, we didn't. In 1997/98 we'd lost only one game on our way to becoming champions, but we could easily have gone through the season unbeaten. We were streets ahead of our rivals. I think Swansea as a club believed they had taken things as far as they could go in their homeland. We had pulled crowds of between

1,500 and 3,000, yet we had played a great brand of football all season. We had a great facility at our ground, St Helen's, bags of corporate hospitality and a number of internationals in the team, yet we still couldn't attract good crowds.

One of the reasons for this, I believe, was because of the success of local clubs like Bonymaen and Dunvant, which meant there was a lot of competition for that Saturday afternoon spot. To try to generate more activity through the turnstiles, the club was thinking of either switching the games to a Sunday or going for a better competition. Historically, in pre-league days, cross-border competitions always drew big crowds at Swansea, and the players who were involved in those days, like Roger Blyth, reckoned we would be getting maybe 12,000 if we were playing the likes of Leicester and Harlequins.

So the club put it to the players: 'What would you rather do this year: play in the Welsh Premiership or play so-called friendlies against English Premiership sides who have given us assurances that they will field their strongest sides on every occasion?' All the players agreed that playing against the top English clubs was the way to go, and the thought of it was a great tonic for us. It was going to be something special as well, because out of all the clubs in Wales only Cardiff and Swansea were involved, so there was something of an elitist aura about it. We just kept our heads down and got in the best shape we could to get ready for a very special challenge.

Within a matter of weeks, the WRU were threatening legal action against us. We were scheduled to play West Hartlepool and Wasps first up, but then we had the Newcastle Falcons lined up. It was to be the newly crowned champions of England against Swansea, the champions of Wales – what a great match! And it turned out to be a glorious day. We had the best and biggest crowd we'd had for a long time. In our last home game, the one where we'd clinched the 1997/98 championship, we'd played Cardiff, yet we only had about 5,500 there. Now I'm not saying that rugby in the Welsh Premiership wasn't good football, but it certainly didn't excite people, and the club and the players at Swansea wanted stronger, more attractive competition. We found that we played better against top opposition, something we proved that season.

The international players at the club found themselves caught between two stools as a result of the WRU's threats to impose sanctions. But I have to commend both the Swansea and the Cardiff clubs because they had competent and persuasive answers for every question thrown at them. All WRU contracts were guaranteed by a third party, who has remained anonymous, and the guarantee was that we wouldn't lose out financially if we went with our clubs. At the end of the day we all saw it as benefiting our footballing careers. I think it came to a point where most of the senior players in the Welsh squad who were involved at either Cardiff or Swansea realised that their main salary was with and their main allegiance was to the club, even though the high profile came with the Welsh jersey. I reasoned that eighty per cent of my football was played with the club week in week out; I didn't want to stand out and back the WRU because I didn't think they were doing everything in their power to create a Super League or British league. Indeed, twelve months down the line we still don't have one.

It wasn't a surprise to me that Swansea joined Cardiff because you don't have to be a rocket scientist to figure out that the WRU haven't produced anything revolutionary to enhance anyone's profitability at club level. Both Cardiff and Swansea wanted to maximise their earning potential as a commercial venture by increasing the numbers of people through the gate and generating income through merchandising etc., and as a result putting a better product on the field every Saturday. It's no fault of the likes of Newport, Bridgend and Ebbw Vale, but they are not big draws, they don't attract big crowds. Historically Bridgend and Newport have been massive sides in south Wales, but over the last ten years they have died somewhat. But for a big club such as Swansea it was a question of saying, 'Hey, if we pull Newcastle, Saracens and all these big guys to St Helen's we could have massive crowds and we're all going to benefit. We'd be playing better football, in front of better crowds, there'd be greater exposure for the players and we'd be creating a richer environment, which is what every rugby follower wants.'

If you asked any of the diehards in the WRU or many of the coaches in Wales they would say that the Allied Dunbar Premiership is not as strong a competition as the Welsh Premiership, but that's a load of rubbish. You ask any player in the Welsh league set-up now, whether they're from Llanelli or Bridgend, and they know in their heart of hearts which is best. We tasted it last year. Some people will say that the league set-up in Wales has been the death of Welsh rugby. I remember watching Bridgend and the ground would be packed. There would be thousands there when Bridgend played someone like Bristol in the Western Mail Challenge. It was stimulating, and of course you'd be playing against fellow internationals and better players, and you'd be testing yourself.

The club had supported us all year, so we supported the club in its actions. We had very tough games against Wasps (beat them twice), London Irish, Saracens (lost heavily to a full-strength side at Watford, by forty points) and Harlequins (beat them at home), all of them sides that finished in the top five. Some say these games were meaningless, but the reality is totally the opposite. Generally we found our rugby far more fulfilling, even when we played against so-called second-string sides after Christmas when many of the English clubs were involved in the run-in to the title. But before Christmas most of them fielded full-strength sides, and they were tough games that stretched us to the limit.

There was no animosity from the players at other clubs; they were totally in support of what Swansea and Cardiff were doing, and wished they had the chance to do it themselves. Even the players from Pontypridd and Llanelli were saying, 'Well done guys, we'd rather be in your shoes than where we are now.' Last season Llanelli and Pontypridd played each other nine times. I was sick and tired of seeing them on television, and that sort of repetition does absolutely nothing in terms of generating enthusiasm. You don't get such saturation in other sports. Liverpool play Manchester United just twice in the Premier League, and St Helens play Wigan just twice in a season, home and away. It was just getting too parochial in the Welsh league – how passionate rugby followers can applaud that I don't know. Wales is a very small, insular place; it's about fifty miles from Newport to Llanelli, and the land in between covers just about every other rugby club under the Welsh sun. As I've said before, I'm a firm believer that as a nation we'd rather see everyone have nothing than someone have something, and that's where the jealousy and carping comes in. Cardiff and Swansea have tried to achieve something; all they wanted to do was have an opportunity to become more profitable organisations, that's all. Ask a guy who has been following Llanelli for thirty years how many times he's seen them play Swansea. Doesn't he yearn for something different? We're all too frightened of change.

Over the last couple of years the Allied Dunbar Premiership has increased its commerciality, attracting a lot of international players and a lot of interest. They're on the right track. They may not be quite there in terms of profit on the field at the moment, but the football, from what I've seen, is of a very high standard. Compare that to the current Welsh set-up. All live Welsh rugby on television starts at five p.m. on a Saturday evening, the worst time of the week to cover live football. I just can't understand the logic behind that, especially in the winter when there's no rugby on a Friday night. Why not put on a Friday night game and then have live rugby on Saturday at, say, 2.30?

I'd like to see BBC Wales viewing figures for matches with the Allied Dunbar teams during the 1998/99 season, and compare them with HTV's from their coverage of domestic Welsh games. I'd be very, very surprised if HTV's were better, even allowing for the fact that for the opening game, Newcastle v. Swansea, champions against champions, there was a bit more of a build-up, and we had this so-called Champions Cup down at St Helen's. We also had live coverage that day on BBC Wales, which upset the WRU. Because it was our first game there were teething problems on both sides, but it was still an incredible game, very physical, with everyone on show, *and* we managed to win it 26–14, so we started off on the right foot. There was a bit of propaganda attached to these games, because every time we were on television, the players were hauled into the club to thank the spectators for their support, because this was the way we wanted to go forward. It seemed to work, because that first half of the season we really got everyone behind us and there was a real buzz about the place, not only in the club but in the town as well, and of course it coincided with Swansea City having a little bit of success later in the season.

For ninety-nine per cent of people watching those matches, and for everyone on the field of play, it was a different game to what the media were reporting, something I couldn't fathom. They never realised just how physical these games were in comparison to the previous season. We were simply coming up against better athletes, and in our first two games, against Newcastle and Saracens, they had some of the best players in the world in their sides. Llanelli have got some great players, and they and Cardiff would generally be Swansea's toughest games in Wales, but apart from them the quality was poor. But now we were coming up against stiff opposition every week. We were in very good nick at that time and we relished the challenge. Of course it meant jumping on a bus on the Friday or the Saturday and travelling away, often staying overnight, but it was an environment the guys hadn't been involved in before, and it was exciting.

When we got to Christmas we put a big emphasis on remaining unbeaten for the rest of the season. We murdered Bath at home and beat Harlequins. When we played Bath the weather was really terrible, so bad in fact that I was undecided as to whether it was worth jumping in the car and going down to the ground. I knew the pitch would be in good condition because it's sand-based and drains well, but it was freezing cold with a gusting wind as well. However, when I got down to St Helen's they said the game was on. A fantastic crowd of around 6,000 turned up, a magnificent effort considering the conditions, which made it all worthwhile. I felt good playing top-quality opposition week in week out, and we were routinely playing on better surfaces too: Wasps and Saracens played on football grounds, and Franklins Gardens, Newcastle's home turf, was a good pitch too. Generally we were playing in front of better crowds as well, so we really relished it.

We had good support from the English crowds, although earlier on in the season sections of the crowd were a bit naughty and there was some real animosity. We were very physical in the first part of the season, over-physical really. I don't know why; maybe it was due to the tension of trying to prove a point. I think things sparked off in the first home game against West Hartlepool, but at the time – mid-September – I was away in Kuala Lumpur with the Welsh sevens team taking part in the Commonwealth Games. It petered out towards the end of the season, but pockets of hostility remained, largely because we had alternating Welsh/English referees; sometimes you'd have Fred Howard and his gang, sometimes Peter Boland and his gang, so their impartiality in the heat of battle was sometimes questioned. But I spoke to the referees and they thoroughly enjoyed the games, which were very fast and very physical. They said it had been a pleasure to officiate at that standard.

As I said, the first part of my domestic season was interrupted by a trip to the Commonwealth Games in Kuala Lumpur with the Welsh sevens team, which was a bit of a disaster really. We were due to play in a warm-up tournament in Singapore along with Australia. I really didn't want to go, but a big sponsored dinner had been arranged in one of the top hotels, and unbeknown to me my presence had been requested there, so I was stitched up in all honesty and had to go. So we spent three to four days there playing in a Mickey Mouse tournament followed by this dinner. Then we went on to Kuala Lumpur for three weeks. Originally one of the Swansea coaches, Kevin Hopkins, was going to take us, and he's a great sevens coach, but then they got Geraint John, who wasn't really up to scratch. The humidity was terrible, and the boys' time wasn't really managed that well. We trained for too long during the day, our fluid levels were all over the place, and of course we didn't get it together and had a dreadful competition. We were even beaten by Canada, and the press made a big deal out of it saying we had been beaten by a bunch of amateurs. I didn't want to take part anyway, because I still had a problem with my neck. I tried to get out of it, but fingers were being pointed at me so I had to go. I didn't think I was fit to play in the centre, so I ended up playing hooker.

The Commonwealth Games itself was a good experience, but we didn't get to see any of the athletics, which was disappointing. It was just a question of getting out there, training, competing in the tournament and then coming home. There was animosity in the Welsh camp from the start, because the rugby guys, about a dozen of us, flew club class and everyone else was at the back of the plane, which some of the athletes didn't take kindly to. But it was WRU policy that for any flight over ten hours in duration we had to fly club class. We could tell there was a bit of bitching going on, but Matthew Robinson was in our squad and he used to train with some of the athletes, so we met up and made friends with a few of them. We had good support from the athletes, particularly the Welsh netball team, so it added insult to injury really that we didn't perform to our capabilities. That was mainly due to the fact that we didn't have the strongest squad. Rob Howley, for instance, had pulled out because he didn't want to go. I didn't have a problem with that because I felt exactly the same, but when Rob turned out on the Saturday for Cardiff the WRU imposed a fine on him.

It's not as if the WRU put a big emphasis on sevens anyway. We didn't have a chance of getting a medal, so I just wrote it off as a bad experience. It was nice to represent your country in the Commonwealth Games, but I really didn't want to be there. Three weeks was a long time to be out there. I'd had the summer off and was gearing myself up for the new season. I was captain of the club, and I wanted to run out on that opening Saturday, but we missed two games, got back on a Thursday and played Newcastle on the Saturday. Along with some of the other guys, I decided that that was going to be the last sevens trip I ever went on.

Captaincy is not something I've ever been too bothered about. I don't put a big emphasis on its importance. Obviously it's a great honour to captain your country, but it's not one of my ambitions; I'm just happy to be wearing the Welsh shirt. In fact I'd already had the Welsh captaincy offered to me, and said no, because I'm too much of a private guy and I value my own time. I don't want to be pestered any more than I am now. But when the Swansea coach rang me at the end of the 1997/98 season and asked if I wanted to captain the club, I said yes. I thought that the Swansea deal was more manageable, I could control the press intrusion a little bit better, and it turned out fine.

I didn't have any problem motivating the guys because they were motivating themselves simply by playing in a better competition. I don't mind being captain, but I did get fed up of shouting, particularly when we hit a bad patch. Shouting's just not really me. I definitely said too much this year; the guys must have been sick of the sound of my voice. I made a point of saying in the last three weeks of the season that I wasn't going to say anything, especially with a cup final coming up, and I kept my mouth shut all week. The duties don't distract me really because there are a lot of natural leaders at the club. Colin Charvis is one – he can take the bull by the horns; Paul Moriarty is an old head, and has a lot of good things to say; Garin Jenkins is the same; so with those three on the field I shouldn't have to say anything – but of course I do.

The way rugby is going now, I don't think there should be one out and out captain who is the sole spokesman anyway. A good team will have a lot of leaders within it. For me a good captain is someone who relies on the responsible athletes in his side, and if they do things right the team's going to benefit. People look at the likes of François Pienaar of South Africa and say, 'What an influential captain.' Admittedly he is a good, positive professional who's also a very good spokesman; what he says does make a lot of sense. But at the end of the day there's a lot of players on the field who have to contribute to the success of a side; a captain can't decide in advance what's going to happen. It's a captain's choice whether it's right or wrong to go for touch or goal, but not ultimately the captain's fault if the guy who's kicking to touch or for goal gets it wrong.

Sandwiched in between all that was going on with Swansea that season were a number of crucial internationals. The first one of that season was on 4 November against South Africa at our temporary home ground, Wembley, Graham Henry's first game in charge of the team.

I'd first met Graham at a meeting I and a couple of the other guys had with him. He'd already met the union officials and all the coaches, and he asked us for our thoughts on Dave Clark, our South African conditioning coach. To be honest the guys were bullshitting him, but I said I didn't agree with what we'd been doing. He appreciated my honesty, and said that he'd spoken to all the fitness coaches, and out of them all Phil Richards at Swansea was by far the best. Up front everyone was going through the same old justifications, but Graham said to me, 'I appreciate where you're coming from.'

To be honest, after only knowing him a couple of weeks he felt like the kind of guy you could probably sit down and have a beer with and not feel that you had to act like a pupil of his. He gave you confidence and made you feel at home, whereas other coaches have been far more dictatorial and schoolmasterly, so he was good like that.

The trials didn't go so well because it was still early in the season. Graham said, 'This is all bullshit. We're going to have to work on this and that.' So he set his stall out from the beginning. But we were on the same wavelength. Having spent a couple of years in rugby league you get to know about professional attitude. This guy had spent three or four months a year with a team like the Auckland Blues, flying here and there, playing and resting, so he knew exactly what it took to tweak a side into shape. He's very much a father figure and everyone gets on with him. He's the only guy in the coaching world I've met who, once the game has finished, can switch off and relax. Many coaches in different sports are still buzzing, still acting like coaches once the game has finished, but Graham's straight back with his feet on the ground. I can relate to that because I'm like that. As I've said before, as soon as the game is over my job's finished and all I want to do is go back to my normal life.

Graham obviously knows the game inside out too, particularly southern hemisphere rugby, which everyone wants to emulate. He analyses the opposition, but in a different way to other coaches. We've had others saying, 'They do this there, and they do that there,' but Graham pinpoints important details, weaknesses in individuals that you can play on, and certain plays that you need to put into place for different games. He went about the preparation for that first international against South Africa in an almost revolutionary way for Welsh players. Under past regimes we'd met as a squad weeks and weeks before the game, but under Graham Henry we got together just ten days before the match. Everyone was fresh and the build-up was very intense but low-key. It was also meticulously prepared and very structured; nothing lasted more than an hour and a half, with a big emphasis on getting adequate rest. More importantly, perhaps, there was also an emphasis on going around with a smile on your face and trying to look forward to the game, rather than thinking, We've done all this work during these past few weeks and I can't wait for the game to be over so it'll stop. We didn't exert ourselves that much, so naturally we came into the game feeling very strong and positive.

The Springboks were coming off a very hard season, and they were already into their last two games. The feeling was that if we could match their intensity for half an hour or so their enthusiasm would die. We came within a gnat's whisker of doing it, too. We began really well and took a 14–0 lead, but let two tries in just before half-time. Graham came into the dressing room and said, 'Do you want to win this game?' We all said, 'Yeah, yeah,' so he told us exactly how to do it. If we had put it all into practice we'd have won the game, I know that for sure. We didn't kick enough, and we didn't put pressure on the corners with the kick and chase; instead we let them run at us and ended up defending all afternoon. Discipline cost us, too. But if we'd only implemented that game plan where we kept kicking long (like Henry Honiball did) we'd have beaten South Africa for the first time. It was all the more disappointing because we threw a hefty bonus away because of one mistake. Of course, a series of mistakes cost us the game, but one missed tackle in particular – by Darren Morris on Andre Venter, which led to a try – cost us our winning bonus, which would have made everyone very happy. However, we got a lot of satisfaction out of the game when we analysed the video later, because we'd played a lot of good stuff.

I relished playing against the South Africans on tour with the Lions where I had a specific remit, which was not so much to intimidate but to put myself about and put in as big a hit as possible. Luckily there were lots of occasions on tour where I did impose myself, but that certainly wasn't the case for me in this international. I got in one or two little hits, but I was never quite in the right place at the right time. I was thankful that Os du

Randt wasn't playing because I had a vision of him having a knife and fork in his pocket ready for me after what I'd done to him on the Lions tour.

The performance of our back row that day gave me a lot of satisfaction; Colin Charvis, Scott Quinnell and Martyn Williams were up against some massive players including Gary Teichmann, who I think is one of the greats, and Bobby Skinstad, but they had a huge game. Seeing those guys getting stuck in gives me a buzz; likewise, if I make a big hit it gives them a buzz. That day the buzz they gave me kept me on a high. We started like a house on fire, but the Springboks weren't as intense on the field as they had been on the Lions tour or in the Tri-Nations. It was our best opportunity to beat them, but we ended up losing it 28–20.

I don't think it was a coincidence that the guys who performed very well that day were those who were playing in the Allied Dunbar Premiership or in a Cardiff or Swansea jersey. The Quinnell brothers, Scott and Craig, were brilliant, Chris Wyatt was out on his own, and people like Mark Taylor and Shane Howarth played well. When you're playing at the highest level you're up against sixteen- to eighteen-stone athletes who can run as fast as you can, whereas at a lower level you come up against thirteen- to sixteen-stone guys. The Welsh team definitely benefited from some of their players' involvement with the English club sides, and I think it has showed in the way that players like Darren Morris and Ben Evans have come on.

I could see the guys in the Swansea team improving week by week. Early in the season Darren Morris was putting in the kind of performances I'd never seen any prop in the world put in. That's because he's a far more open, ball-handling prop than Ben Evans. They are two different players with different attributes. Ben is very physical, whereas Darren is far more technical in his approach to the game, but he's got beautiful hands, more like a back-row forward really. I would hear him inside me or outside me on many occasions, and you don't get that with many props in world rugby. Admittedly that's at club level; at international level you've got to put a bit more weight into the scrum, but they both developed in their own ways, both got selected for Wales, and both have great futures ahead of them.

Just seven days after the South Africa game we were up against Argentina, the first time we'd had back-to-back internationals. It was very important for us to keep our momentum going and our performance level up, which we did, and we won. It gave everyone a boost before Christmas, and I suppose to a certain extent false hopes for the 1999 Five Nations championship.

I think there were some question marks over team selection as far as the pundits and supporters were concerned, but Graham Henry knew exactly what he was doing. We'd played so positively against South Africa, it seemed that with just a bit more hard-nosed experience at that level throughout the team we'd be capable of beating them. I think we'd felt good going into the game, and we'd had a shared responsibility within the camp. Instead of having the skipper talk to us all the time we'd called on everyone to put their two penn'orth in to see if we could all become better people and better players. We'd asked questions like, 'What makes Chris Wyatt tick?' and 'What makes Craig Quinnell tick?' Maybe they wanted an early touch, so we'd tried to marry that to our matchplay tactics, get into the game and be as productive as possible. It had worked well. I'd talked about defence the night before with great passion and in great detail, and you could see there was no fear in the guys. Graham Henry had wiped the slate clean; he'd said you've just got to play with a great deal of passion and huge amounts of intensity, tempo and discipline. He wanted us to play the game flat out, but also emphasised there were times when we needed to kick. When you've got a guy like Neil Jenkins in your side you utilise him, as you do someone like Chris Wyatt, who's so good in the air.

We'd played to our strengths that day, to a solid game plan, which is what we failed to do in the early part of the Five Nations. I think Graham would admit that he got caught up in the hoo-ha of the Five Nations. He tried to dismiss it, saying, 'What's all this Five Nations crap?' Down in New Zealand, if the All Blacks are playing Australia you read about it on the Friday and go and watch the game on Saturday. But people were trying to convince him that the Five Nations was different. But a too-relaxed attitude wasn't why we lost those first two games. We didn't respect the ball, we didn't keep possession, and things we'd worked on didn't come off.

Graham Henry obviously knew what the Five Nations was, but he knew very little about its historical worth and meaning, its importance to the Welsh people. At such a time the Welsh rugby team holds the pride and the health of the nation in its arms; when Wales win the euphoria and the elation is incredible. I'm sure businesses have a happier and more productive work force the week after a Wales win, but I'd like to see figures for absenteeism on a Monday morning when Wales have lost. Not because they have hangovers, but because some people in Wales are physically sick and can't face work after the rugby team has failed, which translates into incredible pressure for us.

We played rugby in ten- to twenty-minute phases in the Scotland and Ireland games, matching the quality of the stuff we'd played against South Africa and Argentina, but we just didn't put the game together. We lost those two on the trot – 33–20 at Murrayfield and 29–23 at Wembley – and of course then we were the baddies; the pressure immediately fell on the coach, and I don't think Graham had been under pressure like that in his career, mainly because I can't imagine Auckland went through many games where they turned in bad performances and had two losses on the trot.

As I said, Graham had tried to dismiss the historical status of the Five Nations, saying, 'It's just a game; we'll prepare like we normally prepare for a game,' but ironically, and unbeknown to him, we prepared for the match like we used to prepare before he came. We trained twice on a Monday, Tuesday, Wednesday and Thursday, and then had the Friday off, whereas in the pre-Christmas internationals we'd trained once every day, rested up in the afternoon and went into the game feeling very strong. We went into the Scotland and Ireland games thinking we were strong, but we weren't; we'd gone through all this technical bullshit during the week but didn't have the shine and the polish. Steve Black, the team conditioner, said, 'Graham wants it like this, but it's not what I want to put my name to.' We are players, and if we're told by the coach to do something, we do it. A lot of the players would say to Steve, 'Hang on, Blackie, I think we're doing too much this week,' and he'd say, 'I agree, but we have to cover this,' so we ended up being on our feet a lot and it just took that little bit of bite out of us when the matches started.

I think we thought we could beat Scotland and Ireland anyway, so we went into too much detail about the way we should play instead of relaxing. Scotland scored soon after the kick-off through John Leslie, but that wasn't a problem; we played poorly, but we still had a chance of winning the game until the last five minutes, when we folded and Scott Murray touched down. We didn't show any mental toughness, and I think it was because we had done too much work in the week and reverted to the old ways. It was a question of 'we haven't covered that, let's do it' instead of 'let's talk about it, we know we can do it'.

I think Graham learned from the experience. For the game against Ireland at Wembley, we realised their pack was very strong and we needed to sort it out. Blackie said he thought that before the Scotland game everyone was too calm; 'I'm not used to that. I'm used to a more vibrant, worked-up changing room,' he said. He thought that's where he'd let everyone down, which I disagreed with. So for the Ireland game we all got a bit too worked up; we went out and gave away a load of penalties and soon found ourselves 26–6 down. We raised ourselves brilliantly in the last half an hour, but lost narrowly. There had to be a compromise somewhere. I spoke at the dinner after the game, and I just said that we had to keep faith in the qualities we'd instilled in ourselves, and prepare for the massive task ahead of us.

By the time we got to the French game we'd changed things round again: very little training during the week in favour of concentrating on getting everybody feeling positive and strong about what we had to do. We went out to Paris and put in a great performance, winning the game by one point, 34–33, our first win at the home of French rugby since 1975. We played some very bold football, although it was nail-biting stuff at the end. We played the same way in Treviso prior to the England game, beating the Italians 60–21. We did very little work, but talked constructively about what we needed to do. We were mentally focused, and that helped us play good rugby on the pitch.

Before the French game everyone was on edge, but there was still composure. It was an incredible day. It was Wales's first visit to the Stade de France, and the changing rooms there were huge. France's back five were all flankers, so we thought if we could scrummage well we'd have a chance. We wanted to be bold at the start of the competition and throw the ball around, but it hadn't quite happened in the first two games because we hadn't performed in the way we wanted to up front, but things clicked in the French game. I got to captain the side in Rob Howley's place for the last ten minutes, which was great, because I could see everyone getting uptight and on edge because the scores were so close, and then starting to smile a bit as Neil Jenkins put us ahead by a nose. When the French got a penalty in the last minute of the match, we were on that line praying Thomas Castaignède would miss, which he did. Then Shane Howarth caught the ball, and I thought, He's going to lamp it upfield! 'Hang on!' I shouted, then the referee said, 'You've got a minute,' so we just wound down the clock and won it.

I'd had some real drubbings in Paris, and that was my first win. It felt great. We'd really worked hard for it, and hung in there. In the second half there wasn't much scoring, but we showed real resilience and character as a team. There was an immense feeling of satisfaction in the changing room because no one had given us a hope in hell. There've probably been some great Welsh teams who have gone to Paris on a high with two victories under their belts and been beaten. As I said, I've been in poor sides and got hammered, but I could tell when we trained at the new ground the day before the match something was different. Everyone was silent. You usually have some noise, but we practised for about twenty minutes and everything was so slick and fast. I thought, This is good.

After the game we went back to the hotel and had burger and chips – you always want a bit of stodge after a match, and it went down a treat on this occasion. You've never seen a room of rugby guys so quiet in your life. Then we had to go to the official dinner. I don't really like them; they are long, laborious affairs. I think the days of the after-match function are petering out really. Both committees get together on Friday nights anyway; Saturday night is only servicing the committee again. The players certainly don't want it. In my view it would be far better to have a buffet after the game; it would at least spare us having to put a tux on. I'd prefer to put my jeans on and fade into the background really.

But Paris was crazy that night. I usually go to the Frog and Princess, an English-type pub in the French capital, and meet a couple of friends. There was great support that day for the Welsh, and I lost count of how many people I met the following week who said they'd been in the Stade de France and stood there an hour after the final whistle just crying.

Next up it was England at Wembley, and I knew that if we were to do anything against them we were going to have to start well. The biggest game is always against England, and that year everyone was wondering whether Guscott was going to play, and whether Jonny Wilkinson was going to play at outside centre. We were strong in the scrum, and Graham Henry had said that was where we were going to slaughter them. He'd said, 'That Garforth's an impostor. We're going to work him.' And we did. Neil Back is an exceptional athlete and he was all over the park, but we did some real damage in the scrum. Our weakness all year had been our defence, but we thought that if we played the right game and targeted and pressurised the right people, we could win. At outside centre, instead of Wilkinson England played Barrie Jon Mather, who is probably more used to inside centre because he's a rugby league guy, so we thought if we isolated him it might put us in a beneficial position. It didn't work during the match for some reason; for us that day it was a question of discipline, keeping the ball in the front five.

It was disappointing to concede so many tries, but the match is, of course, famous for a final-minute move we'd never practised, and one which to this day we've only ever done once, but which at

Wembley that day resulted in my scoring a try against England to deny them a Grand Slam in the last ever Five Nations match. Sunday, 11 April 1999 has become a date which thousands of Welshmen will remember for the rest of their lives.

With eighty minutes of the match already played, we were trailing 31–24. Tim Rodber, playing in the second row that day, was penalised for a high tackle on Colin Charvis – in that highly charged atmosphere the incident looked worse than it was – and a great touch-finder from Neil Jenkins gave us a line-out deep in the England half. I'd talked with Scott Quinnell during the week about a move which was similar to one we used to play at St Helens. Bobbie Goulding at scrum-half used to use the move a lot. Basically, the forwards would punch into the midfield and then he'd get the ball and run across the field, showing the ball to the opposition before giving a short pass to someone like Paul Newlove coming up on the burst. It could be devastating. Scott and I came up with a version of our own where the back row would be out in the midfield and Scott would get the ball and run across the field, hopefully dragging the opposition with him. He would dummy-pass a few times on the way, and then I would come charging through at an angle, take a short pass from him and hopefully blast through the defence. We talked about it, but as I said, we never actually practised the move. We were all knackered when we got to that line-out, but I said to Scotty, 'Call it.' He did, and it worked like a dream. Most people know that when Scott's running with the ball he doesn't usually pass because he's so strong he just steamrollers through. I think the English tacklers were content simply to pile into him as he was moving across the field, but just as he'd committed the defence I took his short pass. If you hit a short ball at an acute angle with everyone drifting from left to right you're going against the grain; everybody else is off balance, so I was able to step inside about five tacklers on the way to the try line. It really made me look good.

Everyone remembers that try, but of course to win the game we needed Mr Calmness, Neil Jenkins, to land the conversion. He did, and we took the game 32–31. I lost count of the number of people I met afterwards who had cut eyes or arms in slings, injuries they'd sustained while celebrating that victory at Wembley. People were still celebrating a fortnight later.

Playing at Wembley was great. It has been a good second home for us; in fact, I felt that there had been far greater support for us there than there had been for the last couple of games at Cardiff Arms Park. Maybe it was because there were true supporters in London, in the sense that they avidly loved their football and were willing to go out of their way to travel across the country. For Cardiff Arms Park matches a lot of people in Wales will have their tickets sent through the post, or they pick them up as a matter of course, and they probably don't appreciate the game because they are pissed up too much. But at Wembley we found the support vocal and genuine. I suppose you could put that down to the acoustics or the size of the ground, but I don't think that's the case; you just get a more loyal and knowledgeable type of support when you're away from home. Wembley's not the easiest place to get in and out of, and most would probably have spent the weekend up there, so we had true support. If the new Millennium Stadium hadn't been ready in time for the World Cup, I don't think anyone would have had any complaints about carrying on at Wembley, because it's definitely a great place to play.

We could have gone to Villa Park, Anfield or Old Trafford, but I don't think that would have suited because they are different areas, and I think the support would have been different. And Wembley has been good to me. I started there on a high, winning the

Challenge Cup final with St Helens in 1996, and finished on a high by beating England in the last ever Five Nations match.

And something of a resurrection of Welsh fortunes on the rugby field followed that Five Nations championship. Beating England gave the team the confidence to travel to Argentina and win a two-Test series, something no side had ever done before, and we ended up winning ten matches on the trot. No Welsh side since the turn of the century has managed to do that – not even the great sides of the seventies – so it was quite an achievement for all those players who took part in the run. It just showed that Welsh players have as much resilience and skill as anyone. To have beaten France twice, England, South Africa and Argentina during that period was quite something.

But when the 1999 Five Nations was over, there were still things to achieve on the club front. Although Swansea weren't in the Welsh league that season, we were still allowed to participate in the Swalec Cup. At the beginning of the season we realised that this was the only silverware we could actually win, so we had that as our goal. We would use the friendlies against the English clubs to prepare ourselves, and if we did that properly then we would surely win the cup.

Normally, a club like Swansea wouldn't join the competition until the fifth round, but that season the WRU said we had to start in the second round, which took up a few of our Saturdays before Christmas. We started against Amman United, and by the time we reached the fifth round we had a couple of hundred-point victories under our belts. It was a pointless exercise. On one occasion we had to play Risca on the Saturday and then travel to play at Bedford the next day. No matter how easy or hard the opposition is, you still have to pull your boots on and perform – on this occasion in the rain and mud. It took a lot out of the lads, but we won both games.

After Christmas we got into the serious stuff, so with the friendlies, the Five Nations and the Swalec Cup games, it was a pretty hectic schedule.

The best final would have been Swansea v. Cardiff; that would really have vindicated the stand being taken by the two clubs. We were the two best sides in Wales, and had been playing some good football, but against Cardiff in the semi-final Llanelli put in a polished performance and beat them. However, we knew deep down that we were going to be far too strong for them in the final, so long as we were disciplined and we applied the right game plan. Llanelli were certainly favourites. They had a better cup record than we did and the press were really blowing them up. I suppose true Wales supporters were behind them because they had stayed loyal to the WRU. I didn't read any of the press reports, but I was getting vibes from a lot of the players in the Swansea camp who were really feeling it and were very bitter about it. It was highlighted at a couple of training sessions we had, and the feeling was definitely present in the changing room before the game. Maybe it played a big part in motivating the guys, but I don't think that was the key. We had a healthy rivalry with Llanelli, and we really wanted to win the cup. I wanted to win the cup.

In the week before the game I was asked, 'Do you think you'll lack intensity because you haven't faced good opposition over the last couple of months?' I replied, 'You won't see a lack of intensity from us. We are in far too good nick.' We'd just had a massive game against London Irish at home which was very, very physical. They thought Llanelli would have the edge because they had played more intensive, purposeful football in the previous few weeks. I disagreed, and I got slaughtered in the press when I said it was men against boys, but on the day it was. Man for man we were just too powerful for them, and we won the game 37–10. I never said that

Llanelli were a bad side or that the Welsh rugby set-up was a bad competition, I just said that at Swansea none of the boys was excited about playing in the Welsh Premier League because it wasn't the best football to play week in week out.

After the game I reminded those present that the Welsh press had said our games were meaningless, but it seemed that on the contrary they were very meaningful, perhaps it was Llanelli playing meaningless games. Anyone who had put on a Swansea jersey that season will tell you, I continued, that the games against the English clubs have been ferocious. Of course some people in Llanelli got on their high horses and started writing to the *Western Mail* about me, but I feel it's pointless being diplomatic in rugby. If you ask me an honest question, I'll give you an honest answer. If some people don't like it, tough.

What really got up my nose was what happened at the Park Hotel after the final. Sir Tasker Watkins, president of the WRU and a lovely man of great repute, took the shine off our win that day and I was pissed off. He played on not how well we'd done but how unlucky Llanelli were because they had played so many games in the previous couple of weeks and must have been jaded. It really took the edge off our victory, and when everyone else clapped I kept my hands behind my back because I felt so disappointed. For a man who was so well respected throughout the game he was wrong to say what he did. Whether he felt it was true or not, he should have applauded our efforts.

On the way home our Welsh physio, Mark Davies, met one of the WRU committee men and he said he was pleased that Swansea had won because it really stuck it to those on the committee who were always sitting on the fence and wanted us to lose.

For 1999/2000 we'd be back in the Welsh Premier League, but surely the setting up of a British league was only a matter of time.

CHAPTER TWELVE

World Cup 99

I missed the Wales tour of Argentina in the summer of 1999 because of a broken thumb, but the tour, as I've said, proved to be a great boost for the boys, because they became the first touring side to win a Test series there. They were understandably buoyant when they came back, and then to beat the reigning world champions South Africa in a half-built Millennium Stadium in Cardiff was another landmark achievement. I missed that game as well because of my injury, and it was one of the few times I've actually watched a match I wasn't involved in. It was a great effort by the boys, and I got on the phone straight after the final whistle to congratulate them.

After that we had a couple of weeks' rest, but everyone was still in a positive frame of mind when we eventually regrouped to prepare for the World Cup. As a warm-up we had three games lined up, against France, Canada and the USA. Of course the pressure was now on, because at that stage we'd had five victories in a row and the World Cup was just weeks away.

To be honest, the build-up was low-key until about a month before the tournament itself kicked off. There wasn't a lot of publicity around Cardiff or on television, but everything we did from then on was geared towards winning the World Cup. Our training and preparation were supposed to be completely different to what everyone else was doing, and this was what was going to help us to win the Webb Ellis trophy.

I suppose I was feeling under a bit of pressure too, not having played since the Welsh Cup final back in May, and trying to come into a side that was winning well. Allan Bateman was playing in my inside centre position, but he admitted that he preferred to play outside centre, and eventually he played a few games on the wing. A lot of people think that the two centre positions are basically the same, but they're not. Inside centre is a difficult position to play. When you speak to centres, invariably they love playing outside because there's more freedom and space. Mark Taylor, my centre partner for Swansea and Wales, is another who doesn't like playing inside, and that goes for the other centre in the Welsh squad, Jason Jones-Hughes, as well – and you won't see Jerry Guscott playing there either. I think playing inside is very much an acquired taste. I enjoy it, because you have more control over the ball, you're involved in more of the plays, and everything's a bit closer to the action. After the game against South Africa Allan said that he didn't enjoy the heat too much, that he liked a bit more of an opportunity to 'show and go', which is what outside centre affords you. So considering all this, although I felt a bit of pressure, I knew that on my day no one was going to keep me out of the team.

My first game back was against Canada at the Millennium Stadium. I hadn't played for nearly three months, but I felt good. We were all a bit ring-rusty because you don't usually start off a season with an international, but we managed to win the game 33–19. It was quite physical – a bit too physical – but we put a few plays together and that got us the win. It was good to get a win under our belts, because next up was France, and we felt they could be dangerous coming off the back of a torrid summer, during which they'd been mauled by New Zealand and Tonga. They really needed a good performance because this was to be their only game before the World Cup. They were also up for a bit of revenge for the Five Nations Paris defeat, so it was a good 34–23 win for us. For the first time in a Welsh jersey I felt that there was no fear of us losing the game. We were under pressure, but it was just a question of soaking it up and moving up a gear, which we did.

We also disposed of the USA 54–24, but for the next month we didn't play any matches at all, which was difficult. We travelled to north Wales, west Wales and Portugal to train, but it's not like playing, and I would rather have had a run-out for Swansea in that interim. Of course there's always the possibility of picking up an injury, but that's a risk you have to take. There were thirty of us in the squad, and although they tried to give everyone a game it would have been good for some of the guys who were probably going to be sitting on the bench for most of the tournament to have had a game for their club.

The preparations, once again, weren't my idea of fun – going on a tour of the country to spread the gospel. The early part of our training in Brecon was fine. It was a tough week. In the second week we were based at the David Lloyd Centre in Cardiff, and we had everything we needed there, so I didn't see the need to travel to north Wales just to do the same type of training, conditioning and ball skills. There was no point to this roadshow because everywhere we went, more often than not, the enthusiastic support of the people got in the way of the training. We'd complete our training run, then it would take us an hour and a half just to get on the team bus. It was ludicrous. When we got to north Wales, it was as if the Rolling Stones had come to town. We had bouncers on the hotel door, there were jerseys and balls to be signed everywhere, and people came from miles around just to catch a glimpse of us. Don't get me wrong, though; the support was immense and the facilities were excellent. In north Wales they have transformed the Caenarfon Tennis Centre into a multi-purpose gym, and they've done a magnificent job and I really applaud it, but there was no need for us to leave Cardiff just to use it.

Perhaps the management thought that because we were going to spend so many weeks in Cardiff during the World Cup it was a good idea for us to get out and about while we had the chance. Well, maybe I'm just a bit more old-fashioned in my outlook. I see it more as a job of work, and the David Lloyd Institute of Sport in Cardiff, where we were based, would have sufficed in my view. Surely one of the benefits of having a World Cup on your doorstep is that you don't have to do as much travelling as the other sides? We'd have only two days at home in between these training camps, which didn't seem that long. By the time you'd done all your washing and organised your kit bag, you were in the car again and heading back to the Copthorne Hotel in Cardiff, where the squad were staying.

A week or so before the start of the tournament the feeling in the camp was good. We were obviously in a tough group; in fact, most of the groups seemed pretty one-sided apart from ours. When we were in Portugal, Graham Henry had announced that the team picked to play against Argentina in the first match would be our first-choice Test side. We didn't have that much depth in the squad, and we knew that if we lost players like Craig Quinnell and Colin Charvis we would struggle.

I was feeling fine, and was selected to play in the opening game on Friday, 1 October, but then I went down with food poisoning on the Tuesday. My wife Sharyn goes to college on Tuesday evenings, so I would leave the hotel, go home and look after our daughter, Olivia. That evening I decided to have a pre-packed meal, and I probably didn't heat it as thoroughly as I should have. Still, I had Wednesday and Thursday to recover, but perhaps, with hindsight, I shouldn't have played that Friday. I hibernated for those two days before the game, and the medical staff told Graham about it, but I don't think he realised how rough I was feeling. I was grey, but I didn't want to miss the opening ceremony.

It was a very emotional day, but because of that, the sticky conditions and the food poisoning, I didn't contribute much to the overall game. The opening ceremony was electric; you could sense the emotion when we got off the bus at the stadium and went into the changing room. Some of the guys went out onto the field, but I opted to stay by my locker. Some, like the Quinnells, were filling up already, because they could feel the atmosphere out there. We had a pretty low-key warm-up because it was important to get the right balance. We didn't want to be over-aggressive or too chilled out, but as soon as the anthem started I think everyone choked up, myself included. I don't think I've done that since my first cap.

We knew exactly how Argentina would play. They would be tough up front, in our faces all the time, and be yards offside all the time. Their defence was a basic man-for-man system, which is considered prehistoric in the modern game. When they were in their own half they just kicked the ball, something we'd noticed from the games they'd played in Scotland and Ireland prior to the World Cup, so we just counter-attacked. The game wasn't pretty, but it was vital that we got a win, and we did, 23–18.

I'd had all sorts of drugs to try to clear my colon, including some heavy-duty antibiotics, but an hour into the game I just started to shut down. I couldn't walk another step. Mark, our physio, knew what I was going through, and that I was totally dehydrated. When I got back to the changing room I just wanted to go home and chill out. I hadn't eaten anything since Wednesday evening, and it wasn't until the Sunday that I managed to get something down, and that was only a bowl of soup.

Having got that one over and done with, we began to look forward to the next game, against Japan. We needed a big win against them because we knew the final placings in the group table could well be decided by points for and against, and I felt I needed a big performance to get over the disappointment of that first game. It probably took me another five days to get rid of the effects of the food poisoning, and by the following Saturday I was feeling a lot better. It was a tough game, but we turned over a lot of ball and were always in control, and by the final whistle the score was 64–15 in our favour.

The next game, against the Samoans on Thursday, 14 October, was the really big one. During the week of the game I think too much mention was made of our likely quarter-final opponents being Australia; there was too much looking ahead. As a squad, we always said that we would never lose a game because the opposition wanted it more than us, but that was what happened against Samoa. They beat us 38–31. They were far more hungry and committed than we were, and even though we had a couple more days' rest and recovery they psyched themselves up really well for the game. We'd lost Colin Charvis, who was suspended after that first game against Argentina, and Scott Quinnell, who'd been suffering from a groin injury, but it didn't have an adverse effect on the squad at all. We genuinely felt we were forty points better than Samoa on our day, but we didn't really follow our game plan. Like most sides who are feeling a bit confident, we tried to play a lot of football and probably didn't kick as much as we should have. That's what won Samoa the game. Steve Bachop, their fly-half, kicked really well that day, and of course they tackled well. I was feeling very disappointed, but I had friends down from St Helens for the game and they had a great day. We ended up having dinner together in the evening, and I used that to try to forget the horrors of the day.

In the papers, a lot was made of my clash with Va'aiga Tuigamala, the Newcastle centre who was scheduled to play opposite me, but he ended up playing on the wing and I found myself up against George Leaupepe. I caught a shot from him about twenty minutes into the game, and as a result I was lightly concussed. He disguised it well though; it was only when I looked at the video afterwards that I realised he must have come flying in with an elbow. I didn't want to say anything afterwards, but with the citing rule and all these camera angles now, there's no way you should be able to get away with dangerous play like that. I told the squad doctor that I was seeing stars but I didn't want to make it known that I might have concussion, otherwise I would have had to sit out for the mandatory three weeks.

As a result of losing to Samoa we had to wait until Saturday and the result of the Argentina–Japan game to find out whether or not we would top the group table and go through to the quarter-finals automatically, so after the defeat the mood in the camp was terrible for a couple of days. We'd got unused to losing over the last six months or so, and were getting to enjoy it. Graham Henry said that as a nation we accept losing a lot more readily than the All Blacks, but I disagree with him. He doesn't know how I feel after we've lost a game.

We took a day out to analyse the game, a day which included a real heart-to-heart session where everyone was asked to be honest. Everyone was, to the extent that we found we were digging ourselves into an even deeper hole. But we managed to turn that round and ended up feeling positive, but it was proving difficult to exorcise the horrors of the Samoan game. A bad mistake had led to Steve Bachop's try, and a mistake in the line-out had led to another. Finally, there was an interception try. So we actually gifted them three tries, and they only really created one. That was hard to swallow.

During the week that followed the inevitable happened. Graham Henry took me to one side and asked if I really wanted to play against Australia. I said, 'Of course I do.' I knew my performances in the tournament thus far had been disappointing, but you don't intentionally go out and play like a prat. Nothing seemed to be going right for me, and I just couldn't get out of that groove. Graham said, 'If you carry on playing as you have done, I'm going to have to replace you.' I knew I couldn't try any harder, but he did more than hint that he might drop me for the quarter-final against Australia.

He didn't, so on Saturday, 23 October I lined up to face the Wallabies in the Millennium Stadium in what was to be our biggest test so far. It was such a huge game for us and everyone was really focused, more than I'd ever seen them before. The press during the week had been quite scathing about our team, which of course we used to motivate the boys. We had the reports in our team room and they wound everyone up. The preparation for the game went brilliantly and the atmosphere at the stadium was electric. There were thousands of supporters in Cardiff – in fact the support throughout the World Cup was outstanding. I didn't go to any of the other venues, but I can assure you that in Wales the attendance figures were fantastic. When the band struck up and the crowd started singing before the game, it was almost magical. I'd never heard a band and a crowd in unison like that before. Usually the band are too fast or too slow, but on that occasion they were spot-on. It was as if they were all singing in a school assembly. It was magnificent.

If we were serious about winning the World Cup, we needed to beat Australia quite convincingly. The weakness we'd identified in the Australians was at the tail of the line-out, so our plays were geared towards exploiting that. We guessed that they knew we usually threw to Chris Wyatt in the line-out, so in order to confuse them we targeted Craig Quinnell more. Our main strength throughout the tournament had been our scrum, so we thought we had to maximise that, although not to the detriment of everything else – an oversight which had cost us the Samoan game. The Australians were very powerful from the outset and scored an early try through their scrum-half George Gregan, but we clawed our way back into it thanks to three Neil Jenkins penalties. But the difference between the two teams showed in the last ten minutes when the Australians demonstrated the ability to think clearly under pressure. That was when our line-out started to creak. Three different people were making the line-out calls, and the ball started to go over the top, allowing the Australians to seize the initiative. I'm not attributing blame to anyone – we are all accountable together – but some stupid calls were made. We desperately needed to get some good field position, to play the game in their half and try to inch our way back into the game, but we just weren't able to.

I think the referee, Colin Hawke, left a sour taste in most people's mouths after his performance that day – it was obvious when we saw the tape of the match that their last score certainly wasn't a try – but the Australians were very strong on the day. Even though we knew they were going to do it, they managed to manipulate our scrum throughout the game and put us where they wanted us to be.

After the game there was obviously a lot of disappointment in the dressing room, although those guys who hadn't been involved much were relieved it was all over. I could understand that; at least they could now go back to their clubs and have a game. Others said they were going to have a break from rugby. I was upset because with a bit more luck we could have beaten the Aussies and gone through to the semi-final. We'd definitely improved for that quarter-final game, but I didn't see a big enough improvement for us really to mount a serious challenge for the World Cup. At least we went out to the eventual winners.

I was first into the dressing room, as always, but my dad was a bit put out by that because the rest of the guys had stayed on the pitch to salute the crowd. I said to him, 'We lost, Dad.' I had clapped the crowd because I thought they were magnificent; not staying on with the others didn't mean I thought any less of them. They'd been brilliant, and they always will be, but when a game's over to me it's just finished, and I just want to get back to the changing room, relax and get home. I've never been one for looking back and analysing games. It's my view that if you don't perform and contribute on the day then you can forget it.

Thankfully there was no immediate rush to do anything after that game. We had to go upstairs to the after-match function and then have a bite to eat in the Marriott Hotel, but I went back to Bridgend. It was my friend's thirtieth birthday and I wanted to be there. The timing couldn't have been better really because I didn't want to stay in Cardiff. It was absolute bedlam there that night. So I went back to a nice quiet restaurant in Bridgend and saw a lot of my old friends, and that finished off my day nicely. I was disappointed that we lost, but after a defeat I need my mind to be taken off the details.

I got up early on Sunday morning and was in Cardiff by quarter past seven to get all my stuff together and check out of the hotel. Most of the boys were still in bed, and it was then that I realised the fairy-tale was over, that I was going home, back to normality. John Eales, the Australian captain, summed up the sudden-death nature of knockout football when he said before the game, 'If we don't win today, then we're back home on a Qantas flight tomorrow.' And it really is as simple as that.

After about an hour of that game against Australia I'd tackled their flanker David Wilson and aggravated my old thumb fracture. I'd stayed on the pitch, but I went for an X-ray the following Monday. It was inconclusive, so I went again for a CAT scan on the Wednesday. The surgeons at Swansea said they weren't happy that the fracture had knitted together so they put it in plaster again.

But what really upset me about the whole World Cup experience was that all summer I'd been feeling great, very fresh, strong and sharp, yet as soon as the tournament started I felt lethargic, and a lot of the other guys did as well. Whether we peaked too early I don't know, but the zip certainly seemed to have escaped us.

My overall impression of the World Cup is that the tournament is now just a massive vehicle for generating income. I was certainly disappointed by the fluctuating ticket prices, which at times were £40, £50, £60, really up and down. I think lessons can be learned from the lack of support in Scotland. And I think the tournament direction has differed. As hosts, we didn't play the current holders South Africa in the opening fixture, and there were a lot of poor games in some of the groups, but overall it was a good experience. It's certainly been great for the people of Wales, and great for the city of Cardiff. Six months before the whole thing kicked off there were question marks over the stadium, but it was ready and it has withstood all the tests. There was a question over the turf, but all new stadiums have teething problems like that, and it'll be rectified. I think the stadium's a magnificent one, and I'm sure a lot of businesses flourished during the month of the World Cup. Cardiff was a great host for all visitors.

On the playing front, no British Isles side reached the semi-finals, and I'm sure England were disappointed because they really believed they could go further. It was the same for Scotland. England played with a lot more fluidity than Wales, Scotland or Ireland, but Scotland were disappointed with their early performances, as we were with ours. I think from now on the Six Nations championship needs to be played at a higher level of skill and commitment. Italy will soon realise that they need to put up a better show to warrant their inclusion.

Every year officials and players seem to agree on the best way forward for the game, yet here we are four years down the line after the introduction of professionalism and we're still missing real quality. I mentioned earlier the ability to think clearly and quickly under pressure, and that's where the southern hemisphere sides beat us every time. The Super 12 competition instils that into them. It's a blueprint which has been proved successful over the years, and in all that time we haven't managed to put anything like it together.

I think the clubs are proactive. They've got a real sense of progression, but you just wonder whether there's the necessary will or desire on the part of the unions to do something about it. It's clear that all clubs in the northern hemisphere need to play rugby at a better level week in week out. That has to be achieved at club level because that's where rugby is strong in England, Wales and France. I believe there needs to be a European league, and I'm sure there'd be no problem funding it.

I also think Britain is searching for a second sport. We've got soccer way up there at number one with all its razzmatazz and pulling power, and in my view rugby is the only other sport that can provide viewers with that kind of excitement. There's a real opportunity there. I'm sure the administrators have got documents inches thick saying 'This is how it should work', but as I said, nothing's been done. I'm in the last year of my contract with Swansea and I want to play at the highest level. If we're going to play in a domestic league again next year, that's no challenge for me. Even at this stage in my career I need to know whether there's going to be a British league or something more substantial to get my teeth into.

On the international front, I'm sure we've got the desire in our squad to be a bit more successful in the Six Nations than we were last year. Love it or hate it, the tournament is an institution embedded in the rugby calendar. Most of the time it's not exciting to watch, but invariably it's nail-biting.

Despite the disappointments of the World Cup, I think the Welsh team has made progress. After the Australian game we sat in a circle and the management said their piece about being privileged to have been part of the group. Graham Henry got up and said words to the effect that even though we lost the match we had exceeded his expectations in such a short time, which shows he's seen some merit in what we've done and had some rewards in the fourteen months he's been in the job.

What we really need as a side and a nation is to win the 2000 championship and preferably a Triple Crown, or even a Grand Slam. That's next on the agenda.

Postscript

Obviously rugby takes up a big part of my life, probably more than people realise. When you're not playing you need to be resting or recovering. My rest and recovery periods are mainly spent at home with my wife, Sharyn, and our baby daughter, Olivia. I don't get to see my wider family that often – maybe once a year – and that's something I'll address when I retire from rugby.

There's always plenty of things I should be doing at home, but my ideal way of relaxing is listening to music. I love listening to jazz and reading about it. I'm into anything that's got a musical overtone to it, but drummers are my particular thing. My dad played the drums, so we always had drums in the house when I was growing up. He was probably playing four nights a week at one stage, so that's where I developed my affinity with the instrument. I used to listen to all his old records, particularly the early albums of Buddy Rich. I'd try to slow them down to find out how they did things, like left-handed single-stroke rolls. From an early age I've subscribed to *Rhythm* magazine and *Modern Drummer* to keep up with the scene, and they influenced the type of music I listened to. It can be jazz, blues or whatever, but I tend to be heavily influenced by who's on the drum throne.

My interest in drumming made me appreciate other musicians, like guitarists and saxophonists, particularly the session guys. When I'm on tour or just away from home I invariably pick up a local paper to find out what kind of music is on and try to go and watch. I love it. I wish I was as competent a drummer as I am a rugby player, then I could scratch out a living playing drums. Rugby's always been my first love, but I wish I'd had more time to practise the drums over the years. I'd enjoy being in a band that just plays around the pubs. My brother, Simon, plays in a band and he has a great time. I only wish he'd been able to go to music school when he was younger because he's really good.

Music has always been in the Gibbs blood, and it's something I'm passionate about. One year my brother and I went to the Brecon Jazz Festival, which was only up the road for us. Simon and I had our picture taken with Steve Gadd, who is a legendary American drummer. I gave it to my brother on his birthday. It's an absolutely brilliant photograph. I often look back and appreciate what pleasure that guy's given me with his music.

I like anything I can do alone, actually. Sometimes I just jump into the car and go down to the lighthouse at Nash Point. I can sit there for hours just watching the sea and thinking. When my rugby career is over hopefully I'll be able to spend a lot more of my time doing all the things I enjoy. I used to go fishing because there's a real sense of solitude in that, but I haven't been much over the last few years. Travelling the world to visit and walk the great mountains is another ambition of mine.

Although I'm still a full-time rugby player, I do have another job. It all came about a couple of years ago as a result of a chat with Rob Davies, the financial director at Swansea. I told him I was married with a family now and my priorities had changed. I was enjoying my rugby and could cope with the demands quite easily, but I wanted something new to stimulate me and I asked him if he could point me in the right direction. Rob, who is also chairman of a property development company called Liberty Properties, said, 'Leave it to me.'

Six months went by before he called me in to meet his partner, Philip Morris. Philip said, 'We're on an aggressive drive through south Wales in the property development side of the business. Simon James, my colleague, has been doing it on his own and he needs somebody to give him a hand. I fully understand that rugby is your primary obligation, but I'm sure you'd enjoy it. It could work alongside your rugby and then hopefully flourish when you retire from the game.' It wasn't a job which was specially created for me, though; Philip has no involvement in rugby whatsoever, but still he thought it was a great idea, so I've been working for Liberty Properties when my rugby commitments allow.

Liberty is a regional property development company based in Swansea and Chester, so we cover south Wales, the south-west, north Wales and the north-west, and are involved in all kinds of developments from an 80,000-square-foot site for Tesco to a 5,000-square-foot property for McDonald's. It's a bit of a mixed bag involving industrial, retail and office property. I work on the development side, acquiring the land and getting the operators involved. I work in the Swansea office, which has a different kind of remit to the Chester office, which has a bigger population on its doorstep. Opportunities for development in south Wales are quite scarce, but when we find somewhere it's very beneficial for the community. We've got a lot of projects on at the moment, including two very notable landmarks in Cardiff which we are developing and which will increase our profile.

I get satisfaction from looking at a specific piece of land which in twelve or eighteen months' time will have been developed into something worthwhile. Last year we sold one of our parcels of land to Cable & Wireless in Swansea, and that created 1,200 jobs. When you're part of a management team that's brought 1,200 jobs to the area, you feel a sense of satisfaction and fulfilment, especially so because you've taken a piece of land and done something with it without ruining it. We're not in the business of developing for the sake of developing. It's got to be right on everyone's terms, particularly as the government are very strict about greenfield sites. You're never going to see housing developments on heritage coastal sites, which is good.

My new job has provided the stimulation I was looking for. I'm still not looking forward to the day when my rugby career comes to an end, but at least when it does I can then work full-time for Liberty Properties.

I haven't had any thoughts on when I'll retire yet. I think my next contract will be my last, and everything depends on that really. I've always said that I'm not really interested in coaching, but I think there's something deep inside me which tells me that I might get involved at Swansea. I have talked about it with Garin Jenkins. I wouldn't be a great technical coach, but I know how to run a football side and get the best out of the guys, get them enthused and instil in them a desire to play every Saturday. The days of flogging guys for hours on end in training are gone. You learn through experience about how to get the best out of individuals, and I think I'd be pretty good at that. That doesn't necessarily mean I want to be a full-time head coach though. It may be on a part-time basis, or it might entail being part of a management team. Of course the opportunity may never arise at Swansea, and if it doesn't I don't think I'd be interested in coaching anywhere else.

Once I make the decision to retire, then I'll just thank everyone for their time and walk away. Of course I'd spend Saturdays with the family, because at the moment rugby takes up the weekend and you're still feeling the bruises on Sunday, which doesn't help when your family wants a day out. I wouldn't ever consider dropping down a level and playing for fun and a few pints; for me, rugby's got to be for real or not at all. If I can't play for Swansea or the equivalent I won't bother. But hopefully I've got a few more seasons left in me.

As far as the national team is concerned, I feel that we're progressing as a squad, but I don't think the commercial arm of the WRU is really maximising our potential and generating a real identity, which is disappointing. At the moment it's the Graham Henry show. He's got some great ideas on how to run the team on and off the field, but as for the WRU, they've provided everyone with a magnificent stadium and they think that's all they have to do. They've got to get their act together. There's an administration problem in rugby at the moment. They seem to be taking their time coming up with a blueprint for a new league. In the southern hemisphere there's the Tri-Nations and the Super 12s; everyone's got their own identity and it's very powerful. We haven't got that here.

A person I do admire is Peter Deakin, once the commercial director at Bradford and Saracens and now chief executive of the Super League side Warrington Wolves. Look at the success he's had, first with Bradford Bulls in the Super League, then with Saracens in the Allied Dunbar Premiership, and now with Warrington. The guy turned those clubs around, and it's not all down to money from owners. It's initiative. He's got his own thoughts and a personal vision. He had, for instance, the foresight to go to the USA and see how the best teams are run. What he's done, wherever he's been, is to bring the club closer to the community and engage in more of a partnership with the town. Just look at Swansea now. We've got a football club and a rugby club. There's a lot of resentment about the success of both clubs, yet we should be working in partnership with hotels, landlords and all the retail people in the area because if the Swansea clubs benefit then everybody benefits. That's how Peter has generated the enthusiasm wherever he's been, and he's doing it at Warrington now. I'm sure the place will flourish.

There's long been talk of a Super League franchise for south Wales. In my opinion, for it to be successful it needs to be financially stable with a long-term view. If Super League was eight years old now instead of four, I'm sure there'd be a pretty healthy set-up in Wales now. What you need is players people can relate to, like Iestyn Harris and Anthony Sullivan, otherwise, as in most franchises, you'd struggle to find British-based players and have to recruit Aussies. Although they might do a good job, people can't relate to them as much.

I think Super League needs more clubs because it needs to spread across the country and have representation in Wales, maybe in south-west England as well. It's still too parochial; it needs a wider audience. In Wales it's all about money and having the right people involved, and that can only come from television. It's a sad state of affairs, really. You see rugby league clubs and their players working damn hard for everything they get, yet it's virtually handed to most rugby union players on a plate. But that's down to a hundred years of history, I suppose.

I think the ideal scenario for south Wales would be a club drawn fifty-fifty from Cardiff and Swansea, although Cardiff could sustain a club on its own because the city is flourishing at the moment and there's a lot more investment still to come. And you can't just import players and expect them to survive; you need a conveyor belt of talent, so you need some investment in youth development in south Wales too, and of course that goes back to the schools really. If it's not played in schools, you're struggling. The game has got respect in Wales, and there's enough knowledgeable people out there to promote the game properly, but you need good financial control, good coaching and good development work, in addition to having good players.

I'd love to be involved in something like that. If it came about, and the right people were involved, I'd put my name up for it. But it's probably ten years too late already. Rugby union is now professional, and clubs like Cardiff and Swansea are trying to break out and do their own thing. After spending the 1998/99 season playing against Allied Dunbar Premiership sides rather than Welsh sides, both Cardiff and Swansea are now back playing in Wales. I don't know about the politics behind the decision or the influence the Welsh Rugby Union had, but I think it's been agreed provided the unions get together and thrash out a plan for a British league by next year. We'll have to wait and see.

But we're back in Europe, and that's where the best northern-hemisphere competition is, the best prize money and the best football. Phil Richards, our conditioning coach, gets us in good nick, so we tend to peak at the right time and be very strong at the end of the season. Hopefully we'll be in a Welsh cup final in 2000, or even a European final.

This will probably be the most competitive year in British rugby for a long time. We've got the Six Nations championship followed by the quarter-finals, semi-finals and final of the European Cup.

Wales aren't touring in the summer, and I don't think many of the national sides are either, so the players will be able to have a good rest ahead of the start of a new British league. That may well be the saviour of northern-hemisphere rugby.

I hope, too, that they look at changing some of the laws to make the game a better spectacle. I think the offside rule should be amended: instead of being the back foot of a scrum or ruck it should be another five metres back. That would give everyone a bit more space, and perhaps we'd see a few more games won by skill of hand rather than heroic defence. This would have to be policed by the touch judges, of course, but then I'm all for touch judges and referees working together, especially on things like offside because a referee can't see whether everybody's onside. Often a referee will blow up straight away if he spots a player offside – you don't even get a warning. I think referees should be more vocal and personable. It's in the interests of the referee and the players that they're contributing positively to the game. In rugby league, the referee and touch judges combine well over things like offside by maintaining lines of communication with the players, and it really helps the game.

My contract with Swansea is up at the end of the 1999/2000 season. I enjoy my football at Swansea, and I enjoy the people and the craic with the guys, but if the club can't satisfy me contract-wise I shall be looking elsewhere. My options include playing in England or France. I've had opportunities to play in France before and always said no, but I'm always one for a challenge, and if that's where the challenge lies, that's where I'll be heading.

Index